DUO POEMATA:

ILION—A TRANSCRIPTION & ALTERTUMSWISSENSCHAFT

IVAN ARGÜELLES

LUNA BISONTE PRODS
2015

DUO POEMATA:

ILION—A TRANSCRIPTION
& ALTERTUMSWISSENSCHAFT

Cover art and book design
by C. Mehrl Bennett

First edition, second state
ISBN 978-1-938521-19-5

LUNA BISONTE PRODS
137 Leland Ave.
Columbus, OH 43214-7505

www.johnmbennett.net
https://www.lulu.com/lunabisonteprods

ILION—A TRANSCRIPTION

Άλφα

I recognized the woman in the window
but I didn't know who she was
just so one world goes away
and another one comes into being
    the flash of her teeth

"Gerusalemme sconoscente ingrata"

the beast incarnate   scaly wings
    aloft in the *shining* by day
come forth from the Scaean Gate
bronze helmets and bucklers radiant
the plumes parti-colored on top waving
in numbers like waves of the tempestuous sea
angry the roar from deep within sleep
    her smile like that of *La Gioconda*

in the clearing above the mill of thought
where hover two seraphim bright that sing

these things that I heard in my head
so loud and confused a clangor as of arms

rushing in phalanxes toward the shore line
where awaited a phantom in size and stature
a goddess

a dream in the seed sown in sleep a distance
cloud like arms to receive what can never be

and to the waters briny brought horses and

two-wheeled chariots to offer to the gods
such sweetness as

depths that in my head swirled as if to never
wake again to spend eternity in drowsy swoon

a poem bedight appeared to me inscribed in
crystal and flagrant ore words great unknown

how to disentangle them to make them recite
obverse reverse and singularities of meter

resound then the seas in the shallow ear!

and if I saw her again in the window
would I still not know who she was
who in the sea of being alone I recognized?

in the mass of details that constitute memory
in the plethora of distinction and definition
that burden light the color of her hair
bordering on rust   the flicker of her fingers
against the glass pane   like rain

-stitute memory the plethora of her rust the
color of hair -stinction and light the burden
bordering on –licker against her fingers like
who she was in the window of being
                    gloves of sleep

sown in the sea dreaming great billowy masses
waves of them proceeding dusky beings from
the Scaean Gate oracular whisperings green
as if to measure against the furious black tide
the army of ants the bastion of porous stone
a signature a word over and over again a

sand a syllable in the plural of resentment
immense tumult the air was full of chariots
and horses tearing the clouds apart the dust
a furor of shields clanging and earth moist
with fresh blood the running against the fray
a water of dreams came rushing over the words
to use a display of works burning treacherously
indignant the night with its minuscule and like
rabies in a pack of dogs the reddening a lust
of emotion and fright, turned to me with her
jade wet eyes

compare them to stars burning out even as
we stretch the body over the clean damp grass
and extend the mind's brief foray into the dense
holding to nothing as in a fever that passes
though a childhood and leaves the thing dry
clinging to nothing taught to detach the self
a spirit seems to fly out from the mouth,
zzzzzzzzzzzzzzzzzzzzzzzzzzzzzzing

the field where magnetic thoughts rally to
what is it, to dismember memory?

filches a crust of bread then runs through throngs
reciting words never before heard or known
a form of salvation emptying in the ditch the sallow
liquid vomiting finally and the lights overhead
the voice droning a mantra of pure hobson jobson,
was not aware of the frequency of emissions
everything tumultuously dark, the never

and if it was in my head, if it was I indeed
the unsurpassed volume and the extinction
of so many celestial bodies in a trice
reeled from the

forced to the ground listening to the whiz
of projectiles above my head
all for, a woman

the shadows that populate night

Βήτα

each who has the other for many and wondrous
darkly the steeped in slumber profound by sea's
edge and sand the various in heaps piled rich
bedside by the turning grieves aloud the weeper
dampened clothes has fixing to clouds thunder's
reckless moan under shoals weaving blindly
how harsh the dank and daggers in hand move
do consternate dream sweeping the who cannot
from such depths restrain and forth rush hot tears
the wildly spurned mind that is in its film rewound

white is it aloft?

many mannered the light a spectacle recalled to what
which is in passing the bright once and gone for seems
an eternity ago in a single blade of grass an inch of rust
a finger whose evening is stanched in a distant sun as if
whorls of dust and the thought conveyed multiple stained
like warrior hordes spent dreaming in a mound of loam
that it was life the extract of bright pressed against a mouth
firmness yielding moistly to the fabric spun despite whole
sequences of error the math of untold resentment and dolor
oblivion it is too soon and fortune's totem beast which would
and innocent too the asbestos poured between the lines
to blanch a blank sphere halved for seeming entire

so the two friends went on speaking by the river bank

dangerous isn't it the encampment of night in mired dust
to heave to a pole and register distances from wall to wall
beseeching pray tell the goddess whitened by eons of dismissal
sectioned and quartered in a heaven doesn't that require
some portion of earth or rain deepening in pillows sacked
by consciousness even as the spear cast by fate finds its eye
in the very center beside the quivering asterisk next you'll
tell me the part about the worm and the middle of things
small friable falling apart at the poke of a pin and darkness
the all spreading its curtain right in the hour of brightest
and spectacular the screen where displayed the multitudinous
and elephants and tortoises and any manner of deity reddened
in the quite abandoned planet wholesale slaughter by the
articulated to mean warfare and justice passion convoked ire

heavy the moody intransigence

dear the darkened when you went and forgot to mail the
ether and Rodrigo parried his shaft no longer burdened
by the earthly personal plunging into the massy welkin
hands aloft the grip of nothing plummeting like black salt
hypnomachia they call it subversive vowels afloat winding
around the unfixed shaft when you returned by day fall
such as it was the floors were amiss the dining set diminished
model planes en route to Africa dear you acted too soon
the letter rewritten for the nth time and addressing the
summit Olympian consonant shifts provoked you again
retreating with something in mind like the
regions designated for their watery zone
and talking sleep wise a subjunctive
wary about the direction given a-
nd driving a cloud vehicle like
gods steering destiny's feath-
ers absence in other mast-
ers a name for missing o-

bjects for grass unmown
hasps of thickening a
legend in wisps of
whitish pale a bl-
ush her faint

the glare

's all a dream fusion of entelechy and the remote
music projected against the waning fan of space
unable to place where it comes from where it's going
rushing out of the main portal in full gear the sons
of Priam one hundred shouting each in his own dialect
responding to some eerie war cry in their collective sleep
aiming to down the oncoming flanks of brazen greaves
head first in the wave of inky directionless or perhaps
tuned to another radio and listening for Ares to arrive
his bright red signal a sequence of hexameters

the great cloud of language

in profusion like cataracts and the many semblances
of man and mask personae personas mumbling half drunk
speech acts of and astounded and benumbed that doors
open to brains and brains seize the fine light only to lose
dense and inarticulate who was trying to write the letter
who was trying to send it the inactive participle the resonance
amaze what is a woman in the list of ships and the lapping
waves of and sandy wastes behind the sphinx and the voice
the Voice issuing from the small pharaonic ear like a story
yet to be invented let alone told to the sleepers in their tents
who restlessly remove one after another their limbs
their short smocks their night caps their pipes and smoke
to return as infants to a
mystery to a house whose interior is the sheer red apse
of a theorem a quaternary shale a designation in litmus

collapsing as all   listing awash lost in the brink
the vast ocean that surrounds but does not touch
Gaia

moon mere memory

Γάμμα

the bright come through *shining*   what is *a*?
snatched her he did and away with her
across the wine dark et cetera   tremulous
among so many sleeping to distinguish the who
which is a boat whose hull lapses against the brim
a dreaming section of it is deeper and darker than
and the loss of so much language and the dense
the intent to marry despite incomprehensions and
the futility of all earth-based enterprises in the scope
of light descending through the small aperture
like a camera lens taking in the freight and wearing
across the mountain ridge and held her tight there
where wind and wailing and the crescent lunar orb
diminishing can we ever say why it is called tragedy
if it is mostly sleeping and the character flaws
idioms of valley and bosky interlude the hatches
many the residents who have capsized in a thimble
the personal and underwear the drowning in so little
calling out in some hill dialect to the god of pronouns
the honorific and steeped in a thick carmine dye
issues forth Legend in her escape clause of echoes
dainty stepping between the white and forced to vomit
it is a wonder we are here standing on this soft promontory
a hissing from underfoot a mattress leaking mephitic gas
here, and down she went all rags and bundles

struggling to see through their sheep do dreamers beware

do mythiform creatures sally forth fully employed ringing
brass quadrilles the session of a daylong hour at noon
the Sicilian meridian when rock and cove meet dallying
a fair song implying with its masses of wind sucked hair
the fair Angelica or doth Mandricardo hold the sway
I can never say emboldened to repeat the many spondees
alas the verdant and the primrose and the budding rose
each a tale to spin a lie to grieve a spouse to misinform
lovers who at the gate pining their tangled minds implore
by Dionysus if this isn't the single most intense and blank
and weep against the steep quarry their rock bound
fate is it the cloud warp of many a distant history
feet of sand and a hand that moving mysteriously shapes
air into all manner of people talking silently to the blue

women skilled in weaving and ornamentation you shall have
to accompany you to the other earth and to hold in your hand
a distaff and by your side a harp to sing the lonely nights

in the labyrinth of sleep: confused alleyways rotting cities
gates torn from their hinges and above all dead warriors
come looking for the bright hemisphere where once

distant tones shifting as the music that circles the planets
one by one and in number unknown and the window frame
and the potted geraniums and the flexible spool of air

when did you ever recognize in the glass the

broken syllables fomented in song oriental a loud echoing
white on white across the thunder torn rocks that form
the center of the world and shading slopes a remote where

woken at an ungodly hour and sent on their black steeds
into the morass a dazzle of speeches and foreign sounds
the ear wrecked by a sacerdotal roaring to summon a god

pronounced lightly and then not at all the immense silence
the otherness of the bleak side of the moon when was that
ever a conspiracy to remount the oracle on its tripod and
flames suddenly at the core of the poem a recital of blind
whose never reaching altitudes and the voice on and on

why is there a fastness above the bay and the deep waters
faceless that evoke the final voyage soundless oars
striking against the pale   like her cheeks

listen and listen again
shrill the unseen birds osprey or lapwing
circling in the mind's obdurate fog

is it to arouse the Muse with some choice words about
memory salt spray wrath and finally death

?

a fuse a fugue a

           Δελτα

foam the sourceless summer froth lapping sleep
fickle bubbling shhhh ing whoosh gulls screeing
wing slap slapping against Poseidon's azure wind
rushes quickly to enter the dreaming the darkened
succession of days without idiom the unconscious
witless the anomie flapping against wet cloth sails
forth sally the myrmidons from depthless beds
hypnomachia struggling with a music voiceless
yet sublime in the key of Delta nacre and sapphire
then turns to winter's gale a stone weight a dank
oppressed sheets mouthed in stifling when portals

---

slam th'endless dark what skies have never seen
and in masses thick the fray now long underway
the under tow the seething tide the restless wave
how far the window glimpsed away it seems undone
do all things conspire to one end? does Sokrates
in his basket survey the many world phenomenon?
ocean swell and god-birth in rocky heights aloud
what matters the dream-portent the muffled roar
that through the earthly seams implores divinity
vertiginous text of the stars numinous counterweights
fate's countless and uncounted threads torn asunder
do dreaming thoughts write these senseless lines
and sway intentions to take the city of far-fame
in a single night walls uproot and gardens blast
'til morn finds in shambles the glitter of brains
the dust of mortal reckonings scattered in the air
it itches to recall the how when why a whitened hand
a phantom's pulse declared what then is *she?*
some ghostly ink wavering in the mind's blank eye
then what the hell says I let's take her by surprise
in phalanxes forty deep the insect horde proceeds
midges mites and flying things that bite in clouds
of day make a midnight's hapless rosary of blood
blindly shapes the camera its human designations
by no known name the enemy cadavers in the street
pandillas roaming swarm in colors fiercely deep
surges like an ocean storm and howling torrents
stir the mix of preternatural things in cold flame
through gore slosh and mangled frames crying pity
whose ear no cortex holds whose sight slings light
into its paragraph of unending space and AOI
does end this transcript do others shake the fray
do sleeping microphones deceive the edge of sound?

this is thick the ancient bark a verse a threnody
through waters vast as what has never been and lo!

her it cannot be she phantasm of unfinished sand
who shimmering swerves through shoals of zero
into what nether paragraph into what dense wood
inscribed with necrologies of the famously unnamed
whose wounds are these no balm heals whose sores
running at the mouth whose purulent mind-trough
fashioning the thought serpentine into its deadly coil
I lapse from conscious fire into the eddying stream
far below the courtroom's hemline far beneath
the world's shallow currents a fish without syntax
a flitting shot of light between two human ears
still this song conceived I pierce the empty husk
and shaking frills around her deathly form appeal
how numberless the gods behind their empty door
do then and again come dashing forth like imps
the universe to confound in ire and contemptuousness
here hold the unseen banner and twill the reedy note
we lose today what tomorrow would not contain
a planet a girl a leafy moan a starfish a mirror
no more the gusset and tarnished flash of lies
to live it was once the thing to breath to breath
again and

crystal rills the earth like glass do run
rivulets in sleep conform to other lives
and waking which is who you ask
drinking to slake oblivion's obelisk
that shaking needle thin as motley air
and in the eye its spear drills through
to consciousness yield the dark drive
and waking which is who you ask

fragments in the key of Delta
the many and numinous notes aspire
               liquids of sun
motes

> penniless the mind
questing in the lonely gyre
to in the woman delve
> how much is lost
cannot be grasped the hand
> falling as the body does
from its celestial parapet
> to inky pools of endlessness

and waking which is who you ask

έψιλον

wrestling in their sleep the two Ajaxes
and Diomedes the huge   primordial ooze
of consciousness the pinprick of light
day surprises and the enormous grey welkin
descending toward the oneiric cavity
fosses ditches moats ramparts walls
cities ten deep slumbering one upon the other
palaces submerged in the morass of tangled sleep
labyrinthine dream of girls like cigarettes
pirouetting over onyx floors speaking jabber
and from the Hesperian distance the sea song
a whistling of contested winds in the small shell
held to the deathless ear
> tomorrow will be different
it says in the small ledger in the temple of Hera
hard by the road to Halicarnassus
in their yellowed sweat-soaked sheep
wrestling   the greater earth
> the lesser earth   who was
naming things never before seen
who was placing carefully the incense brazier
who was not yet awake yet talking talking

something about the other life the stranger one
bucklers and greaves and helmets
a peacock's cry out in the middle of nowhere
a courtyard empty but for the clay urns
filled with an indecipherable circular script
and the small drizzle of ennui in the drain pipes
smoke from a distance hinted an encampment
the roster of ships   of women left behind
in dormers thick with perfume and sperm
rose water sprinkled in the obscure mirror
where memory of a face fades
someone yelling departure the full moon
still atilt in the western rim
who remembers *that* who recalls the shudder
weighing anchor the drowsy head of slumber
falling from the body immemorial   the

it will all come to naught   islands
floating in the verger
                    blossoms like syllables
spelling a magic name
but here in the ditch folded over twice
the mind in its perpetual narcolepsy
fevered thoughts fail to grasp and javelins
sharp flying objects boomerangs
catch in full flight the unwary soul
Hector!   who dared one and all
to single combat   would Diomede or
the Ajaxes twain not come forth tottering
 all the rest is written in backward Minoan glyphs
tortured spirits flung head first
into the narrow crevice called Hades
what aping gods with barking heads do laugh
watching the mortal spray make air incarnadine
somewhere else cliffs stand erect in their siesta
geological shelves morph intrinsically into heavens

massive cloud banks release a thousand years of hail
no intelligence is there to register the trajectory
of many-thundered lightning the gift of Zeus
hurled from his Dordonan bower
reclining drunk beside white-armed Hera
and thousand-headed ants swell the lists of helium
that circle the variable and dying planet
this is a sleep within this sleep and shifts of red
layer the multiple city where lie unfathomable
mythical heroes drenched in the shower of fear

a single mind has this conceived
written on one leaf over and over
it starts in darkness and revolves into
another darkness repeating the same
but never ending the same tale
an excursion into the Unknown the baleful
who tossed the dice who drew lots
who won the stolen girl who lost her
fighting fists flying swords drawing blood
I found the leaf with nothing on it
of itself the writing happened all at once
repeating itself in circularities of heat
grammatical incisions syntactic occlusions
absence of harmony absence of prosody
I wrote the leaf with nothing on it
it repeated itself writing and unwriting
erasing the blanks creating the blanks
issuing forth from an exhausted vein
the tumult and cries of a thousand dead
naming them whatever I could imagine
burying them digging them up again
putting words in their mouths
sewing up their lips sealing their ears
the *Sirens* with wings of molten wax
shrilled the epithets I had long forgotten

I crumpled the leaf I tossed it aside
it came back at night crawling
it came back at night crawling
it was war between red and black ants
it was unrecorded miasma and code
it was the repetitious phraseology
that brings heroes to the unwilling page
that engenders gods beneath the lintel
it was the work of a single mind
a madness dappled contraries fugues!

    Ζήτα

consonant clusters afternoon migraines
listing against the monarchy of sand for hours
light dwindling through the periscope to a few
always the struggle to recall the dream exactly
the was it why we came a shallow disposition
for a, woman, naked consequences a fiction
on the battlements a shape haunting of paper
figurine in the manner of lost numerals
the severed head still talking in the dust
with its diminishing memory of tamarisk
while all else in a swirl vanishes from sight
aphasia amnesia oblivion night's realm
stuttering the human animal in the dream
distance is all the main floats away in fog
lapping waters break the stillness of time
when mountains had wings when smoke
was the word for heaven and there was
nowhere else to go but inside the stone
that marked the boundary between sleep
and death and listen intently to the din
in the earth above the great *hypnomachia*
hearing tales of illusion and deception

a, woman, at the heart of it the presentiment
of windows and shattered air lunacy
the invention of dust and of the body
that proceeds from dust and the body
politic and the stain that spreads over
and in the midst of so much rushing
the madness of weaponry and bloodshed
enormous bodies of shadow howling
that no one has where to go afterwards
lost in the labyrinth of ancient water
sleeping in layers beneath the bone works
massive iterations of a once glimpsed sky
revolving in the forensic eye of a midge
cataleptic sessions of sleepwalkers
the insane reverie
distended myopic horrific blind
in his remaining eye deaf to the purulent
gnawing of inwit Zeus chief of the gods
lends no ear to such mortal travails
yet stalks earthly denizens motels
units like aviaries perched on cliff's edge
hungry for girls and wives alike capable
of doubling himself at midnight and
of sleepwalkers groping for a leather
armrest for a pepper shaker for rain
whatever seems tangible palpable
eye of a midge cataleptic sponge flies
sessions in the midst of rushing weaponry
buzzing of the immortal in the porous rock
to listen intently for the next debacle
numbers going backwards from the fount
shepherds stumbling like sleepwalkers
dovecotes beehives the ideal landscape
to go home to that battle weary
fixing to kill for a lie for a phantasm
a, woman, whose irrepressible beauty

impressed in wax for the moment only
led us astray through consonant clusters
through the rhetorical maze of the city
whose constitution belongs to flies and ants
the monumental perdition out to sea
a hundred shapes shimmering at noon
the colossal hour of total destruction
Sirens Scylla and Charibdis Circe
the wanton who spit at the crossroads
bringing down the moon at midday AOI
circling the volume of heat where it is
written no man will survive this one
      no man will survive this one

    Ἦτα

passing as shadows through insect forests
bitten scourged driven wild by incessant buzzing
the myrmidons, us, we , not them, sleep-stalking
inimical alphabets moon stones planets out of orbit
ringing in the ears interred in liquid bronze
speech impediments baggage of unwanted phonics
stoned on blue lotus fused to sand the tongue
the hour of sheer immobility sun struck clangor
looking for the bodies we left behind, we , us, not
them, *terribilità* of the psychopomp in his Egyptian skin
aglitter like a wet snake   *Hermes hear us out*
Hermes hear us out   lead us shaky figures, us ,
across the forbidden water , across the forbidden water
make for us oblivion the sweet passage , for us ,
Hermes we beseech you recall for us the day,
recall for us the light, some light   we are fallen
today we are fallen into the sleep of bronze, Hermes
hear us out do not leave us face down, mud is a
dream and insects devour us stinging and itching

the universe of skin and youth Ah Hermes are no
more, us , gone from the realm of clean air and
sky above and clouds like signals, us, Hermes
conduct through the portals of grey dust through
the realms of the forgotten   today we are fallen
and swiftly does memory of name and title go
Hermes   Hermes take your caduceus and
strike the waters   let the two serpents part darkness
for us, us, we beseech you   Hermes for we lie
freshly in dark pools and enter the sleep of bronze
unbidden   above our former forms the clangor
of battle zooms and soars   for us no more, us
no more face down dreaming nothing in its original
state the baggage of language released in mud and
from our wounds the dark stuff pours forth never
to return Hermes, us

there comes us a day when donning your armor
and the dust and the flitting insects and the heat
and you don your armor and you know then
that life is worth leaving and the bite of the nettle
and the brief incision of the briar and the sweat
coursing from the temples and you sense you are
no longer yourself not the self in the glass nor the name
a mother gave you nor are you nourished more
on that ephemeral ego donning your armor that
life is worth leaving and death is worth living
inner sanctum green pulse the framed void
words of anomie of anterior lengths of grasses
shadow of infinity the never diminishing inch
within which Hector takes the mortal swerve
us, Hermes deliver across the murk
beseech Thee, psychopomp, let shine
          more   a light , us, not them, face
down interred in the bronze sleep
bright flung red the banner sun's fierce coil
wrapped swart consciousness in blazing metal

stepped forth from the ledge of flame into the

besought with imploring hands the burning orb

air became clouded with swarms of flying insects
in the ditch troops of frogs ranting against the night

the myrmidons, us, we , not them, sleep-stalking
wrestling with enormous shadow beings the harsh
mouth flooding with the bitter accent of immortality's
deep and dark vowel   a talking in the ear
some whispering like sand chafed upon skin
hypnomachia thunder of the horses of chaos

is life worth leaving?

          Θητα

the *pandaemonium* that accompanies
                    the evolution of light
transmogrification   the transmogrification
obfuscation   the obfuscation
the transposition of heads
they come down the hill yelling blustering
the mob of 'em just kids inspired for the first time
by the godhead deep within and arrive breathless
at the shoreline shouting
    Θάλασσα   Θάλασσα
they do not question it's war and nothing more
and have at it with the other gang all unruly
equally inspired and think nothing of the deaths
laid out on a strip of sand and the girls
funked out and falsely pious bowing reverentially
to a bunch of idols painted all pretty and sending

up prayers and imprecations for which side
is gonna win and which is gonna go home busted
smell of incense and mumbo jumbo words
air fills with the intensity of summoned deities
invisible as midges in a cloud-like swarm
   Salve Regina   *Salve Regina*
this beautiful soprano voice makes it clear
that cherubim and putti and small caryatids
all together white are listing in waves of air
atomic particles making the bottom of heaven
all blue and threatening with tempests
of agitated aluminum lightning bolts and afar
mountains seem to sing being aloft with wings
oblivious of the clangor and martial fray below
boys in suits of poorly fitted armor and neck ties
flinging clods and slings and stones at one another
and from the briny depths arises *Thetis* or someone
like her and the hoary distance is filled with *Poseidon*
raging all salty and fulminant with disregard
for mortal lives the little piss-ants smearing
one another with daubs of blood and gore
some have their brains spilled on beautiful rocks
painted to resemble the other side of the moon
others with broken limbs go hobbling crazily
in circles around a monument to sleep
by three in the afternoon it's time for the Greek lesson
and those who can who still have some wits
gather around the simulacrum of fire
prepared to recite in some Oriental dialect
the various hymns to the Dawn and to the Winds
if only they could get their mouths around
the sacred vowels but it's restlessness and curses
blame goes flying like maddened gnats in the air
eyes get poked out cheeks are scratched open
briars and thorns and thistles crawling with ants
eager to have a part in this colossal battle

red and black with jaws wide opening devouring
spears of grass pebbles lichen dark mossy patches
the terrain once holy to the *Artemis* of 50 breasts
now littered with grammar and rhetorical particles
strewn like bits of matter blasted from aerial warfare
to reconstruct a syntax of classical elegance and purity
from this farrago of phonetic disarray and corrupt prosody
instead spit and spattering of false etymologies
faux accusations of lyric meter set to alarm bells
hobson jobson Anatolian pidgin bawk talk nonsense
these guys having at each other on the sandy mount
waves of ire pitch dark at noon fists smiting effigies
ghosts and phantoms of all the *others*
keys hair combs unlikely buds prospects of lies
life lived before it's begun wrestling naked on the heath
winter's eye devolves its storm crescent tides flush
high the again why where and whenever the dying
girls all mawkish and pink in their chrome a-weeping
thick licensed tears and incense of burning fat
to the heavens rising lifts mortal hope to what
the numinous and swerving deities uncaring smite
each on a smooth youthful cheek and down all descend
to Ἔρεβος and there kiss that wan phthisic beauty death
            "deep darkness shadow"

the *pandaemonium* that accompanies
                        the evolution of light

                    Ιώτα

a part of it covered with white lace ,
what you couldn't see and the advertisement
for sky , a flying fortress of clouds flaming ,
dusky combustion , irregular verb forms , a
nevertheless the warnings , too late the indentation ,

the unmarked paragraphs , asterisks and iotas ,
small quivering absences , such was the residue ,
blanks , aspersions , the massive polyphony hidden
somewhere behind the detritus , columns half erected
of parian marble , the sea like an intimation , come to
rest by the olive grove , smoking , captivated by the
sight , marmoreal fluted iridescent the sheer surface
of it , next to that what is childhood , what is a siesta ,
counterbalance of dreams in flight , heat in dense
circles , sweating the nightmare , a black form
manifesting behind the eyelid , where the brain
struggles to translate light into , suggestions , mere
adjudications of thought , a process of foaming ,
of , like the sequence of ants endlessly climbing ,
the thick wet trunk , like a decapitated , in their
eyes , something , is it Spanish , is it Hindustani ,
a woman whose pigmentation is evening , colossal
as dust , leans over the balustrade to signal ,
what , to sign the air with her balsamic fragrance ,
bath oils , sea salts dissolving in the accent of her ,
voice , long narrated columns of pitch , when each
of us also , not them , moving mysteriously beneath
the nocturnal syntax , embolism of stars in flight ,
galaxies that have no beginning flying like , mountains ,
yes, and the hint of corruption in the stone , someone
else is behind the portal , *hypnomachia* , thunder of
the horses of chaos, again in the resident ear , gold
of the moon diminished in ire , furious the rattle of
archaic weaponry , archaeology of the air , spun
round the invisible distaff , palaces full of honey and ,
girls dressed as bears singing paeans to Artemis ,
someone else is writing this , someone else is being
us , not them , when there is a hint of dawn , of the
enormous female entity whose girdle slips from ,
view , worlds come and go , lattice work and windows ,
whom I recognize but do not *know* , to read this text

aright , study hard the correct pronunciation , the
various accents circumflex and grave and acute ,
get up early before the light , plow the fields that
lie to the east , leave the cattle to their own sun ,
because this is a transcription , the original of which
has been lost , like the indecipherable handwriting
in dew , wait for the summons , and the banner
flapping harshly in the wind , knowing beforehand
that home , that you cannot turn back , leave the narcissi
in their plot untouched , kiss the sleeper because ,
nod to the petty deities at the top of the stairs , dispose
of the waste water in the lateral trough , forget whatever
went before , the chapters about ink , about the greater
island , the asylum where sand becomes identical ,
it is a nothing here at the bottom of the page , iota
subscripts , insects waking for the last time , dreams
so enormous and intricate about a single blade , of
grass , long slender stems about to flower , purple
yellow indigo , like heads to be lopped , by day's
infinite end , the charge of dark breath into the ,
fray , memory , one by one the indecencies , skin
exposed to red shifts , the lotus eaters with their
mouths floating , holding palm leaf fans , a moment
of lust , suppurations , already the fleet sails full ,
across the slender arm of water , the distance of
a dun colored cliff , the promise of a bed , however
uncomfortable , to lay down the head on foreign turf ,
and imagine this writing is going on , a buzzing , a whirring
of cicadas in the back brain , the eventual heliotrope ,
the , the , the , instant of oblivion

κάππα
Amor la voce e l'intelletto dona
Boiardo, Orlando Innamorato

disembarked on the other shore for what
fleeting sensation of done it before
chalk fields loose electric outlets uprooted
telephone poles an ominous figure in the midst
echoes of a recent dream about the origins of dust
did you come here to rescue someone?
is it about love? is it *only* about love?
myrrh from Rhodes the finest and a pillow
and blankets and a mattress out in the rain
ghosts parading the main thoroughfare of Mycenae
remembering exactly nothing of a former life
who was admitted into the chamber
who was denied absolution even undressed
and the talk about peace treaties and wagers
unripe grapes divine voices nothing but girls really
swarms of them on the dusky hill slope
color of parched olive a canopy of clouds
descending with a god in the midst
to hash out the details for the coming campaign
a hundred black ships at least and a commentary
about dream interpretation and gold masks
in the eventuality of dying abroad
mists fine as the filtered sands of sleep
a horizon comprised of distance and longing
not sure footed filled with doubt and
when next you see me I'll be six feet gone
the charm of these groves their shady nooks
where to rest the brain from its harried task
composing in longhand the definitive version
the ultimate transcript the numinous thought
what does it matter lost count of the hours
waking by midday to the mournful sound
shaking ever so slightly from the recall
how the water surged in the wake
and the thunderous applause as we set sail
rounding the promontory of hazard

heading straight into the lost sunrise
who were we then in the riot of youth
to undertake this rash enterprise you may ask
who weren't we who didn't we resemble
other than the shadows that glide through sleep
making speech acts under foreign skies
was never here before did never apply
somnambulants passing through rock crystal
as if by some love driven to journey beyond
what was never found the indefinable One
Selene/Helen/Living-White-Moon/Phantomas
we regurgitate names only to find the Unnamable
asbestos aspic blanched blank whiter than pale
immobile yet fluidly stepping on the battlements
nocturnally spurned by Artemis
when yellow was the cause of deception
and turbulent throngs mustered around red
time was a pinprick in the canvas of night
indigo jasmine honeysuckle thyme marjoram
the bee swarms of Mount Hybla concupiscent
dizzying b

      uzzz

          ing

                    hemicranium
pitched into death's Sicilian estate
nymphs the color of cyanide step barefoot
into the depthless pool

    Λάμβδα

the show where the mountain played a part
equidistant from longing and immortality

what is more ancient than red and its polyphonic dust
illegitimate syntax voluble emanations from space

---

nowhere but in the listing mind in its shipwreck
wake of lesions of water enormous depths of sleep
no one wakes to remember the why of the second day
nor the tertiary stone placed at the entrance to the

the mysteries are for women only the disenfranchised
the white that forms around the opaque mouth
of the oracle divining such futures in rock crystal
who are the passengers of light whose memory
is tethered to a thin rope of saliva and the din
that rushes the air with a fury of blank meter
behind the walls beyond the gardens the suchness
elevated to a tone of infinite

beached on the other shore weary sleepless
uncounted moments spent in
damaged goods   exhaustion futility
waves lapping blackness   a rain

when approached the ominous creature
and wherever they stepped and the shadow world
among them none knew who the other was
and sat him down on the hewn throne and
stared back with cold impassive gaze
spoke to none and for hours the smoke
and the tumult of the outer
existence utterly at a loss as to the meaning

the initiates all girls between twelve and fifteen
a huge steaming cauldron on a tripod
and chewing a drug of some kind a bay leaf
eyes rolled back to pronounce in a language
more like the hiss of serpents or the buzz
sultry afternoon heat the island seemed to
float away in a miasmic swarm of dreams
each of them introduced to the mysteries

vowed to eternal silence

poetry is the art of navigating blindly
through cloud swirls of memory and echo
not knowing where it ends nor why the endeavor
unconscious bidden by some crazed mentality
to weather depths of ink singing ever
the unknown

thus it speaks the ear some native bent
yellow descending into loam rich earth

nonetheless facing the mute and ominous stranger
for hours that became days and in the stillness
an eroding silence could hear the hairs growing
and the cave and the inhabitants without pronouns
usage of sterile rites a water held the distance
short of breath the last to arrive none the wiser
with tales of inflicted wounds and an air thick

someone was kept writing this and the scratching
of the quill or whatever against the slate was
it still sleeping from above a voice issued
plaintive and bleeding because it was plucked
hastily but could not mend the torn hem
and the words fused to a rush of vowels
told us to turn back leave the coasts all fog
no map of the land that lay upcountry
how could we in our dizziness a quarry to some
divine madness listening intently to the sign

forever and a day

the letters seemed to waver barely luminous
above our heads the minute it came to be dancing
a music of infinite distances of light and thought

we were given bodies to hold and shape tightening
the screw that drives the pestle moving shafts
and flowers of suddenness and the sense of loss
configurations like the numeral that stands for
whatever it was delivered its mass and went dark
the rest of us shifting uneasily on our feet
with nowhere to stand and the sulfurous reek

IO! IO! IO!

$$\mu\tilde{\upsilon}$$

a mystery is in it
          shipwrecks magic potions
enchantress and the garden of beasts
from the bridge looking down at the
we know them we knew them all
the many dead locked in ice floes slowly
backwards who are speaking our voices
through them the eternally wounded grafted
to consciousness the light an aspect slanting
shifts red into planetary unknowns
is in it   groves mephitic and ghostly
beckoning winter citadels the ashen a
symbolism of sand the names each one
a grain of the pustules of air opuscula
minora degraded in seas of night texts
illegible the heights orographic choirs a
knowledge of green underground dark
wore his armor & spent the apostrophes
rounding what is a flutter the waves a!
snake sight of filched illusion a frame
situates at the apex a letter at a time
short for midweek the next day is dying
who moaning in their sleep capped by

diatribes slipping under hands give way
nefarious grasses of Pluto weeds snatch
the deathless   marmoreal after life
crops of rust latin roots at the base of
when such weathers confine the algorithm to
something less than its personal pronoun
the effect of oracular discord the fray the
immense and darkening days endlessly
why are we here betrayed by gods and demons
like smoke that returns as a phantom of
in one's own bed remembering the light
how it visited the tops of the trees
and the dew with its miniscule alphabets
we are tossed into the midst mud and slings
the likelihood of ever seeing the Citadel
the underclothes of a goddess   moon-like
turn the back towards the and forget the
! smashing illusions in a porphyry of regret
did we get here by teleportation
across preterit and non-existent time zones
the sword the caliber the untreated wound
balm and ichor fused to unseen pain
lip turned out sweat beaded and inch
the flame measures its future by 'whelmed
ants in red swarms hiving over the City
the blind eyes of dust with one leg shorter
than the other the burning with its volumes
of gas the corridors poorly illumined of the
and gods hordes of them making clouds
eating venison at dusk laughing like wine
what is a *thing* in the center of so much noise
a vortex of ! finished off the unique water
poured the remainder into the empty brain
torn from its socket and pitched at an angle
revolving senselessly around the rampart
horse hooves metal glints fossil engines

roaring in the inanity
we knew the many dead they were us
talking through a dandelion stem to a
how many more locked in the chip of ice
a regard for the women who cannot be
whose hoarse whispers inside the lichen
does it appear to vanish is the stitching
of air yes the decibels of fornication
in the remote ear and palisades of shadow
tossed the carrion into the hounds' ditch
once shining heroes with eyes of bronze
the gleaming in the night of
sections break off of the poem the neatly
inserted some parts borrowed from the
and set up on a pedestal the nomenclature
of sand the variable and unending

vv

was pretty the small story about
the wee she thing it was in the shadow
because it is evening in the eye the many
the uncounted hour dusk the dappled
was in her little clothes and crying by a bed
like a stream of planets in her tears dropping
every part has a middle and every middle
has no ending she was on her knees wet
and wasn't it a tower and a buckler
all by midday in the sun glint of an orphan
she was a midden heap of a bliss in her
sleeping outside the eye and darkness
the sudden bloom of starry something a
chasuble or an ornament flickering like
all mixed up the day and weeks like one long
night perpetual inside a box happening

with swarms of midges and flying wisps
crying she was her eyes out and lisping
a prayer swoon to Astarte Aphrodite Artemis
the torn hem of blood the bared calf
running through the crocus and high and sweet
a voice her voice perhaps a throat shining
someone is chasing her some big like an ox
cruel horns and flushed cheeks eyes rolled
back to see the other universe speeding
but in the weeds a song greening clouds
and other what chasing hard hooves sound
it's for all the girls who dwell in mystery
who never come of age their skirts a twirl
in the vermilion vine of time unwinding
her is the singing a flame devouring light
and swift behind the bulking one-eyed
his breath a labor of anvils blue with heat
the circularity of things trespassed once
sad and oriental of disposition the cliff
she clings in dreaming waves a cry a wan
hands detach and letters manifest aloft
neon glimmer the nonsense of *vv* unbound
weaving graces sound a paean to the echo
hill is twilight dun the dusky altercation
drifting in the ochre spate five furlongs wide
comes the path no more and circles fringe
sleep the bedding of tender grass the grief
her was a little tale and married to a yellow
kinglet whose braids of torture rust agape
come tell me this come round me that a hasp
a mast a virgin lingering in the brine a fling
what many demi-gods hiding in the brush
do her espy longing becomes the loud night
brandish club and ivy twined the brain adrift
often the told however much the when and why
words fail to use silences the immense comply

how deep the fall I feel it how she on the rape
a meadow ensconced the shepherd's crook
his pipe did ply the sundry afternoon an air
these stories have no start a sleeper in discord
does ever wake the sorrow needling brow
underground the earth gives way the dense
a darker never was a sounding in the gloom
will pick her up in a trance and swiftly wings
her take to ramparts of the hidden moon
herself the diminishing orb a paling gleam
a distance of too much to understand
how encrypted stars spell histories of dust
where she can step naked in a bath of ink
for all to read her transcript the fading
all too fast
she remains like a little mask with plumes
around the eyes and flickering eludes touch
while in constant flight in search of sands
to make amends//
a sphinx

ζι

words don't have to mean *shafts shiftings*
sounds don't have to make sense *AOI*
hurled the many pennioned dart into his eye
a cosmos unfurled in the shuttered lashes
blood the length of time *without significance*
fell like a boulder into the dust face first
we have over the centuries puzzled over
running the motor *gunning* the motor
winter gasoline pages unnumbered space
turned the leaf over to find a small voice
bleeding vowels infinite as dew vanishing
no one has ever heard that *sound* before

and hungry for human meat the goddess
on the prowl her menacing grey eyes alert
to the least movement in the underbrush a
soul *with baited breath* is it lyrical enough
or she is angry with her torn peplos stained
and gleams in the darkening air her naked
buttocks all puissant glistening with rain
pornography of war *omphalos* and *vulva*
second day after the solstice *teeth flashing*
the narcotics and automobile industries
ambulance wards filled with drifters from
a battle cry the situation is far from –able
when from the ramparts of night a solitary
like a bird of unknown plumage shrilling
and the capsules of the stars break open
wide and turbulent *red-eyed* ants the
! seen from afar like a goddess, *the god*dess,
and stuttering from the horror of it of it
brandishing stripes vermilion and turquoise
like weapons aimed what is that a name for
a situation mingled with ochre dust sunsets
ineffable beauties of the apocalypse shouts
from the groin *spermatazoa* bright as a
confluence of the *Phlegethon* and the *Lethe*
carrying on their backs irregular structures
like verbs or homophones killing fields
distances as when she corrupts the spittle
with whatever the god gave her to swallow
both onerous and numinous an *ignorance*
worn like an invisible girdle *Wonder Woman*
that is, the divine *Diana*, whilom we stagger
in masses of unassembled porphyry enacting
the recent battle plans using termite and chinch
to struggle to pronounce their names let alone
assume their *titles* no wonder there is no end
and search the sky for the Riddle inarticulate

whilst in their tents and breathing hard
to dream silver a stream something shooting
radio signals from the past *illegal syntax* a
that bear no significance to the work in hand
reciting from the margins or footnotes the
memorabilia marching upcountry spoken
sotto voce yielding nothing to the hooded
emblem using the goddess as a disguise half
in the air half fitted out with skin *the song*
numbed we are suppliant and to get that
thing out of the eye the fountains of gore
the littered with remnants of their bones
in shards or tattoos up and down her arms
white-shouldered *Hera,* in the alleyway a
ruckus between two gangs the either of them
blind and using adjectives of *force* whistling
gravel and clumps of weeds sipping from a
thick substance like *ichor* or ambrosia
yes, tallying the number already felled
the mute and inveterate *dead* so called for
their inability to get up from the ground
relying chiefly on a text called the *Theogony*
to get a point across and the missiles of heat
the circular and immense fogs lifting from
recently dug canals cutting across the isthmus
could then see from a selected promontory
the myriad fleets of nightmare churning the
vast waves and the sharp edge of salt
in the dim air and yells and roars and *whoops*
hollering din in the abyss of sleep a dull
heaving his hoary heavy head the *Sun* high
above the eastern hemisphere and eructations
of light semaphores small attempts at meaning
sounds that lack utterance a shrill *Help*
! a transcript of phonetic decay or worse the
disheveled from a night of absolution her

wings her talisman ripped off course a sheer
nylon around her throat abandoned to
and heads straight for the camp of the *Argives*
vengeance and envy at her side saliva
in ropes clinging to her sleek thighs Oh

     Ὄμικρον

hypnomachia the tipping point , or ,
knock some mock sense into them ,
cloud-floaters , drifting all from light
, ancient and tumbling from beds ,
lit the small flares for wayfarers , them
hidden from view , the drill pipe the
hose stem , the invention of fury
I wonder if I'll ever see you again
anxious to have at the rushing shadows ,
to impale them to the flame , like moths
who were the substitute women in the dream?
confusion between ardor and amor ,
insects at best , the railing in silence ,
against , the ones who cannot decide ,
who foment strife and business , who
the spear-bearers , the grass , who
carry each grain of sand , precious
and colorless , a vision of glass endless ,
to choose between what cannot be and
superstitions about odd numbers , nights
when *Selene* corrupted , the occasional
apostrophe , reddening streak in the hair ,
abundance of it , in thick masses tangled ,
hands do not sustain , the aforementioned
the antithetical the undisputed , a coil , a
single strand wet and , cannibal stars eating
their own fate , unpainted gesso heroes ,

what has already occurred repeatedly
barking in the lonely acres , who is that ,
coming on horseback , flashing black glint
, head underarm , lantern aloft , trees bent
as if praying to the goddess of the cistern ,
the again the wherefore and the , why ,
maddened , somber , despondent , ? ,
windowless , isn't it ancient to be so grieved ,
partaking of the moly , on the quest under
earth , Ulysses hobbling toward the ships ,
bonfires guttering beside the dark waves ,
a cleft in the air , I am the strange , a bed ,
falling from one sleep , into another ,
how can we free ourselves from this *sleep?*
sheets , muffled echoes , a plaintive ,
childhood in the winds , weeds , stems
of darkening , evenings spent in mulch ,
to lift even one arm up , to signal with stained
fingers , Ajax mighty Ajax , clouds of heads ,
formations of summer lengths , heat , a ,
to fall again into brassy dreams , a clangor ,
a mission of water , seas rushing from out ,
of nowhere , filling the ear , everything
becomes its own distance , stars of pure
fading , mornings of white absence , can
never be as before , a
sitting here on this promontory beside our
selves ghosts or mutant phantoms talking
in a language of asterisks and parentheses
what can we remember of that other sleep
when we struggled with one another in the
furious exchange of identities
heard as through a small pink sea-shell ,
murmurings , hoar-frost voices , something
writing underwater the same story
a faint , one , or

the

πι

more and more the haze the loss
of rectilinearity and mythiform air
subjunctives of hyacinth and jasmine
perpetuating an archeology of color
gorgeous as you are in hyaline solution
even as buzz swarms around you of bees
menacing inimical critical dark mass
blackening in the sand pools of blood
much like the face you wear or wore
in the gymnasium naked for an instant
before the powdered veil descended
and the summons to another world
embraced to a text of fictional opposites
night accompanied by Legend and Echo
emphasizing the unknowable wrapped
a mantel around your body issuing
as it was from the pronouncements
just so suddenly did youth end and
the alabaster caryatids fell silent

was it half way up the stairs when
        it happened
or the dawn when the girls gathered
        at the well to fill the jugs
were there letters written in the clouds
      dismissing the memories of mortals
or was it the faked silence proclaimed by
      Dionysus consumed by bees
when did the encrypted names come to light
        bearing weapons of smoldering
envy and ire and the injunctions to not

go to fight were ignored
well trained the young bodies replete
    with ignorance and fury
climbing the ladder missed the step
    commencing the long promethean fall
was it on the drill field of trampled flowers
        that it came to pass
and dust and the roiling waves of voices
    young and distant and incoherent
was it persuaded by the boon of immortality
    that the cars swerved fatally off course
it must have been the summer of intoxication
    of heat in sweet dizziness
it must have been the lure of fornication
    with a goddess of choice
in full raiment of white skin and perspiration
        that forced the conclusion
beyond that what else happened besides
    the infernal voyage across the tract
and the ten year siege of the impregnable
        citadel of quicksilver and soot
an atmosphere blackened by flying missiles
        and cries of regret and loss

do I not deserve a place above the earth?

ῥῶ

a voice the color of smoke issuing
from the caverns of sleep
    back to the woman in the window
        back to recognizing what is not known
a river runs between it and everything else
memory dividing itself between white and blank

sheer river between blank and white memory
running a divide and hove to the javelin
aiming straight for the animal whose career
is the length of sleep between it and everything else
animal burrowing into the sands of an anterior life
aimed the javelin straight and HOY! a cry
waking in demise the dreamer of dreams
whose afternoon was spent in the eternity of silk
carmine red abusive indigo clouds bunting
hemmed in by a certain fear and aimed hand straight
the javelin for the animal truant fleeing eyes
the myriad unfolding in the single petal roseate
a dew drop formation of secret alphabets
and hastening the minute territory of opium
coursing through the river dividing white from blank
the rest is a woman an outline in Greek shadowed
on plate glass and the furniture hooded and drowsy
I spent hours in the concentricity of her absence
heated eventualities of a dialogue which occurs
somewhere in the pit of the unseeing organ
vast and trembling jellies of space the horror
of the vacuum interrupted by the unerring hand
that aims in its boundless youth the missile
straight for the holy beast and talking all the time
to strife and envy and the guardians of mortal skin
singing as it were as whizzing the bolt flies unerring
in its aim at the heart of the divine beast *thought*
it is treachery working this poem through its transcript
not naming what should be known and the restless
in their sleep of dread and oracular mouths at the ear
reciting endless logarithms about the time it takes sand
to pass backwards into the river that divides everything else
a hand a switch on the wall a reflection in a small water
grass to the side of the house in the shade of infinity
where insects carve worlds out of a clod of dirt
and within a blind bard chants the supines and gerundives

of an idiom spoken inside mountains and wings
take flight and the mind is a buzz with hives of wrath
a blade of light that cuts through the apex and whelms
cataracts of an insanely transparent fluid
and so much more that cannot be rightly remembered
sitting here on the transept that overlooks the abyss
and listening to the rope tell its tale and the weft and
so much more that is being forgotten even as it is
being transcribed even as it is being transcribed
and the ends of things and the worm at the very center
devouring the fable of silence
does light never take place again?

tiny mouths *Phlegethon*

"love her madly"

    Σίγμα

hissing oriental substratum
pray we to the *Lord-of-Mice*
hauling out our ships rounding
reefs of the unknown and shattering
bricks of memory turned sidewise on the loom
woof and quartered by some unseen Mind
the aggravation of light probing the seismic
how can we ever return to what we once were
legendary and summered by silks of shadow
talking the talk of the other side of the mountain
and issuing from caves and silos and the fountain
where dawn first announced its intention
why didn't we listen instead of idling
with our motors and fauns fanning
the improbable oracular with syllables
torn from the bay leaf the goddess left us

why couldn't we hear the imminent collapse
of our future in story and grammar
going back and forth over the rules of conjugation
the mindless syncopation of pronominal stems
juxtapositions of helium and verdant hours
spent unthinking on an earth dotted with disaster
shaken by a sudden tremor in the spine
nerves cut through by a menacing light
flares gone up over the olympian crest where Hephaistos
welded thunderbolts to the seamless cloudwork
high even higher above a deity with lizard eyes
set to our undoing by sending dreams of midday love
wine and the quivering pulse of the heated ivy
so that by the time the sails unfurled in the airless bay
and drunk or sated with endless foreplay
the girls had their sport with our careless bodies
days passed like minutes in that savage foliage
of sex and duplicity pledging unending *eros*
to victims of illusion and shadow that passed through
us like sieves their delusional but powerful rouge
capsized the crater of thoughts fell into the steep water
darkening for a minute the pellucid surface
for us to wake on the other shore ten years hence
grizzled knotted puzzling over the loose threads
and in our ears the egyptian sistra and cymbal
the tom-tom beat of cardiac irregularity
was this the concussion of Beauty?
was this the storm on the distant Pleiades?
was this what they meant by the *Key of Delta*?
every day is equidistant from death
the weeks we thought were sessions of eternity
born in the grass and lengthened by the cicada's song
that was just the flash of consciousness
between the ear of waking and the ear of passing
what are *words* in this *hypnomachia*?

thunder distance and levitation
divine dreams of the person holding the weapon
sleep walking through the maze of false intentions
come crashing irreversible citadels monuments of dust
orients of sigmatic mystery climbing the trellis of the sun
into the apogee of a lifetime lived in a minute
wondering whatever for this instamatic photograph
taking in all the living dead under one umbrella
exchanging masks and names and thought patterns
elaborating sacrificial rites serpents white oxen
enormous stones erected at the behest of the oracle
watching blood and sperm alike fall like rain
over the cadaverous silence of the day after
when the remains of stone and sand linger
adrift on the celestial sea of alone

pray we to the *Lord-of-Mice*
Apollo himself who shines on these ruins
for love of poetry and song and the Beautiful
and never ending myth of Light

ταυ

in the thicket of it in the dense
I play with my little spear
and galloping the horses of dust
and statues made to look like sleep
the multilayered cloud floating lost
with my little spear on the chase
and the small animals of powder
who dwell somewhere behind the wall
I wonder that so many have eyes
that so many still wander in the dusk
I am a hill a tree a rock a cave

I am water running for my little spear
to hunt the migrant spirits of the stone
to play with each blade of grass
and summon mostly when asleep
the divinity who governs causes of war
and on the morrow ready myself
for life and the chasms of breath
dumbstruck with the passage of light
as it enters the career of my sight
and exits when I can hear no more
but with my little spear and small mind
I can go anywhere in the thicket
I can move restlessly in the dense
on the prowl for what I cannot have
guessing that by day stars are dreams
seeing horses of dust gallop by
and palaces of jade and bright water
suddenly in the mist begin to shift
making way for sun-axled chariots
I think a Nymph is by my side shining
an ornament hastening to go afar
together we fix the dun colored hillock
and claim it is the middle of the earth
but on the morrow I must wake again
with my little spear and smaller mind
on the hunt for what I cannot possess
the powers of love like western winds
the trees ravage and mountainsides
diminish into corroded piles of salt
red ants have the day a banner high
incarnadine silk for a whole afternoon
running through the maze of heat
a quarrel a puzzled spat a fling
her aloft she sings the battle cry
stung to the quick I look about startled
only the peahen in her flutter of color

drums her dance in the solitary moment
clouds like immense hours of menace
the sky consume and me I am gone
threaded through the needle's eye
what of my Nymph the shining
what of her plaintive battle song
now become a mournful threnody
a shaking in the air a sudden distance
whole worlds away my parallel life
resumes its vagrant alphabet of dew
shadows on a painted screen remind
me that I once was here a prince
a little spear some fleeing beasts
the good and true of language
shadowy virtues all a toss in heaven
gods of mildew lichen and smallpox
drowsing in the fetid eastern sun
what of my Nymph the radiant
her embrace a death I could not own
remote the ringing in my skull
slender remembrances of a lawn
too vast the size of ether greening
furtive beasts nuzzling in the brush
a missile thrown a brief explosion
something somewhere gone wrong
statues the shape of sleep dimly seen
in a trance I watch everything come and go
words like rain hail or sleet come down
rushing into the water underneath
who will wake tomorrow thinking
it is I all over again a little spear
in the thicket's midst the dense
a panoply of shadowy wickerwork
masks and talking talking talking
the evanescent figures on the wall
the things a mind imagines

falling asleep one last time

smaller by far the inch of sky
into which the perpetual vanishes

thinking to hold a hand only
                          an absence

zzzzzzzzzzzzzzzzzz

υψιλον

*   for wretched are men*
it is not for them to foresee the future
but only to live immersed in the fog of the present

just when were the Dark Ages? are they now
when error and misfit and ire and vengeance
sway the rudderless bark into dangerous shoals
Aiyee! desperados wearing bucklers and greaves
swinging sharpened iron weapons left and right
cutting to the quick many a living soul
for the least infraction and daring to move forth
darkened by what they saw in sleep the night before
and the monster at the edge of the brain reddening
casts all hope out the window and erects shadows
and embossed silver reflections to the skies
declaring the victory and triumph of What!

snares ploys stratagems cunning and artifice

when the hoary sun lifts himself from his Anatolian bed
and casts his Lamp first obliquely then by degrees higher

over the glassy surface of the Ionian mere
        rock seems to
                        signal to rock signifying the *Shine*
then are we imbued with the Mystery
and in the grotto of the west where Darkness nestles
and the scores of demons without right awareness
and machines engines knuckle-bones bottomless sinks
all manner of Stygian paraphernalia
hoodoo-doll castoffs fright wigs indelible lipstick
war charms on neon display   where Evening
is the same thing as Eternity
                justice is of no consequence
so easy to mistake houses
        the sun rises on the one
                it never arrives on the other

fragrance of red and blue lotus

vendetta against domestic workers
including sex slaves kitchen maids scullery
jack of diamonds knaves of court knife slingers
the ones who at the bottom of the heap
forced to eat human offal grace of the gods
never ending put on notice or fired right off
to the sound of drum banging battle rousing
and the streets paved and unpaved rife with hooves
dust of acrimony shifts in phalanx brass-eyed heroes
descended from cloud dynasties lock-step marching
in a trance to a dactylic hexameter NA NA NA

there are ways of not thinking
of crossing the path of a wayward deity
picking among stones in a heap
as if searching for the moon
some grass that clings to a missing finger
the strange sensation being dizzy and falling

into the shadow of another being
waking dozens of lives later in the Pythagorean gyre
only to discover beneath yards of red dust
the inveterate and inchoate cosmos of Hesiod

a place in Egypt called Heliopolis
burning reams of fictions about the *Origins*
archaeology of sand // inverted pyramids
within which the dead suffer foresight
calling out with mouths suffused with opium
for *Mummy NUT*   star goddess
the untranslatable

then do men in their folly trust to one idol or another
and become angry invoking names sacred or cursed
drawing vengeance of the heavens down on their own likenesses
declaring the supremacy of the god of Unconcern
over the multitude of numinous entities the size of bees
and draw up battle lines and punch and kick and stab
spittle and thin threads of blood line their jaws
and before sunset does their sight swarm with ants
and to the bitter earth they fall forever gone

I say unto You that peace be the prize
but the generations that come and go as leaves
soon forget and rush to the anvils of Hephaistos
steaming and hissing and shaping molten ore
into the simulacra of oriental armaments
Hunh?   formless and almost divine
the Idea of a Higher something and shattered
the body like dry clay to smithereens
and as each holy new year comes around
and men who in their sleep have bitten the dark swarm
awake on mats of dry straw having dreamt
of raiment radiant as alabaster
pull off their old scabs and slobber into bowls

full of the leavings of a sacrifice
defiling with their every breath the Order of things
They it is who forget whence

too much grammar not enough foreplay
the howling in the midst of phonetic decay

of the myriads slain that day
here are the names of a few
Iphthione *his head split in two*
Demoleonte *his brains spilled by a spear tip*
Hippodamas *struck in the spine rattling like an animal*
Polydoros *a spear in the back pierced through the chest*
Dryops *struck in the neck by a fury*

the small voice that belongs to the stone
does no one hear it?

    φῑ

and what of Helen the ageless
in whose sleeping eyes tiny red pigs cavort
rats lice toads all manner of vermin
her unconscious form that of an ant-heap
of Helen the senseless whom moons surround
swarming night-shades bats ululating owls
desire to fornicate with the lowest of gods
the ones who govern alleyways and toilets
the ones who manifest as yellow suppurations
of Helen the imperceptible phantom of
the locative case where absence whitens
and dawn bursts suddenly like a flock of birds
signifying an approximation of heaven
or the deathless fundament of the Hour
no one comes back from no one remembers

of Helen the countless more than sand her shifting
her illusory her luminous her ineffable
her death-defying her retrograde her pallid
her one two three her digitalization her once
her nevermore her sphinx her musical her
her her her uncounted unnumbered unlettered
her spring-box her fumous her snaking her fiery
her sheer her distant her longing her regretting
her upside down her greek her abysmal her
aphasic aphonic unutterable
, when we thought to have seen her again
a mirage haunting , the moonlit ruin , the
sheen of it the very shining through it , a
skinless seemed she a lizard opposing walls ,
darting in the eye of the most recent dead ,
a , liquor of light , an incendiary thought ,
wearing for repose a supposition of naked ,
shoulders bared to the flare , could we but
call her name had amnesia not overtaken ,
and set restlessly waiting at the back door ,
taking a curtain call for the nth time , she ,
then disappeared like a piece of tinsel ,
somehow air , somehow dense , somewhere
else a flitting song , a canon , a round , a fugue ,
an elision after the definite article , summoned
for a minor traffic violation , her blush , her
hypothesis , naked from the ankles up , waxen
figurine embossed on parchment , the seal ,
was no one there to make a report , something
like gun fire in the attic , stairs caved in ,
a muezzin dazed from , the sun's immediate
violence , hematoma , infinite lesions , brain
dead from , cantered like a frisky pony ,
for dreams only , sacked the city for weeks
and a day , ashes , cinder , sky burnt in excess ,
of Helen , of , yes, of night , tears of the Centuries ,

the ,   [whispers]   thunderer
who have in vain toiled , and watched red-eyed ,
the whole up in smoke and clouds , rolling ,
for years , and the bottomless weeping , and such
as have never before seen , nor been seen , wearing
pelts from the north , speaking in disorientation ,
and what of her , the ageless , the senseless ,
the imperceptible , the countless , Σελήνη
bull , rooster , dog , and torch: Ἑλένη

we are come to some midpoint to some theory
of the universe devolving from and returning to
as many as were the boats and the coasts ransacked
and not coming home but through metempsychosis
me changing you for her the other still just watching
trident in hand and roaring with all the force of a
summer fortune a tsunami taking the whole of Ionia
leaving on a few dry peaks bleating the shepherdless flock
abode heaven form taken by midnight inky miasma
confused with the luminous entity Helen devours sand
desperate to have back the godhead
we are centuries from fully understanding
the causes of the strife and are content to ramble
though patchwork excerpts of the transcription
making round the missing vowels and crimson the once
whatever it was of beauty and the shining refulgent
singing aloud though sleeping deep the
to the *Muse*

                χῑ

in that time speaking obscure hill dialects
oblations in dun colored   fragments
        burnt thighs of fat kine
of prosody and mutations of vowels

memorizing ritual phrases passed down
since immemorial   clouds of incense
gathered on the beach in the dark of
tarring the hulls   trochaic
spondees   consonant clusters frequently
colored red the symbol of   visited
by the goddess smoke-shaped and hovering
dare not   lessons in rhetoric and grammar
the unopposed verb   shattered minds
who depicted on burnt clay receiving
as a gift from   the sublime ,
it said in a cursive backhand   shifts
leaping over the fire   indefinable angst
        evenings caught unawares
what few of us remain   alphabets of ink
amorphous inscriptions of sand on sand
is there anything to remember   the iso-
lation   is there anyone to recall are the
tombs empty   to read if possible
what is on the backs of mirrors to read
a fate there a single   asleep as earth is
in the long winter of unending   , circular
histories of air   amphibian delusions a
waking to hear waters rushing on either side
a hand minute rising from the shoals white
waving dactylic   a poems is in there ,
submerged in our own lack of recognition
the window where the woman   who
knows us from somewhere a song the
perhaps of the incidental and unremembered
we all go back like serpents to another time
to the origins   maybe , in conjunction with
some astral projection sitting on roofs waiting
for dawn unencumbered of darkness to lighten
reddening the Anatolian heap   whence
some myth the small words like breath

in the recondite ear   a chance to move again
here among ruins looking for the finger
in centuries of grass   aching and somber
if the hour this one will ever complete
its alphabet of dew and   puzzled
if we look again toward the   lamp
something else indistinct   consciousness
and across the furniture of dust a shadow
     mated to the incorruptible soul
a mathematics of hearing , a   echoes
a tintinnabulation meant to sound aloud
the breaking of   wasteland forget
can never get over it   lying there bereft
of anything like spirit the human   inanity
calling from a sleep of eons for the soft
her quizzical shape disintegrating as motes
against the glass   horizons more horizons
longing and distance and the little
some colored others without quality
floating just inches above   dark portal
steps that descend to Pluto's throne
smell of benzene and diesel fuel   roaring!

here you will lay the sacrificial and light
pay no heed to the suppliants women they are
rent garments hair torn a glass shard begging
for what the god will never yield act of possession
simulacrum of the world of the living slowly
burning the rich fat simmering for hours
weeping in each leaf of the laurel branch
and hold high the smoldering rod the spike
speaking the unremembered speech of mountains
for the engine of trouble has come to visit
and the unfolded diameters of loss and
for some time you will be cast in oblivion
nothing of this must come to pass nor bright

of day resume its circle

ELELEU, IOU IOU

Ψ_1

colophon and caryatid acanthus and cornice
the inexorable structure of sand and distance
goat-song the tragedy of coming home unlit
measuring by the verb *to be* the ineffable longing
dying unawares in a foreign dream unspoken
plaster-of-Paris Psyches Aphrodite in a bee hive
sanctuaries for the floating dead in a nutshell
camps abandoned on the littoral smoking high
inching in and out of each unprescribed letter
the worm whose craving gnaws the shape of thought
is *never* too soon?

round the bend darker waters never shored the light
haphazard moving through *hypnomachia* raw shapes
crying out against the brassy shield of time small sounds
aging and defenseless in the archaic folds of Echo
what are there words whenever out there the empyrean
ablaze with sonant clusters of ire and knocking knocking
hard the bone shatters into a million stars knuckled
refulgent spraying out into the form of a poem or
shards of language splinters of vocables lodged
in the brain of fever dragging penitential shadows
around the city's vast and walled circuit in grief
where ashen figures recite nightly the paean to blood
shafts that uphold the planetary ellipse though shivering
and wounded all fall down mouth full of night blooms
eyes devoured by a race of red and black ants swiftly
to hurry memory to its outpost high and swart oblivion
with a murky water flooding the inch of space earth

its daughters pawned for bouquets of ancient marvels
a face an immense broadens the moon's violet trim
seeing through the mass of ornament and gilding trumpet
inspire dreams awry their inky alphabets spell days
when illusion is without end the enormous grass the
spelt and millet and corn and rice rotting in broken
painted the surface a bright to inform the shadowy
they are still talking in leaves that cluster at the apex
which is a form of kingship lying under sheets of coriander
to understand the valuable of circumflex and acute AOI
so many rendered lightless this is a threnody for it all
them unrecognizable mutilated rusted with gaping dew
a recall of the sweet a thigh reveled by lace torn wide
a significant holding her faint white arm into the cloud
where buckler and helm have their speech and a role
spreading its stain across the brief lore of consciousness
miasma palace halls darkening transepts Ionian and Doric
gates of pure stone erected to resemble the sleeping Sun
whose cattle a shame we eat unmindful of the dross of death
fungus reveling can we not come back Hey is that a voice?

when all doors are alike and the shape of night
the flux in the ear a distant roaring the remote
call of the god whose reverberation is a loud ore
islands below they come and go shuttered by bright
when did Calypso and Circe and Nausicaa?

a trembling shifts its ochre into a pale
noon once a swarm with the buzz of light
no life returns, Friend

and held the unlit and endless lamp
against the empty vowel

exit Psyche

Ωμέγα

on the chronometer it is no time at all
unless it is ending
others in the dark a surfeit of oblivion
madness to wake charging at the invisible
in search of missing organs and windpipes
the long siege that was supposed to cure all
nothing but a sandstorm of confusion and
whatever else there are not enough bodies
to justify and all the prayers and sacrifices
unless it is ending
and the Wheel of inexorability and the changes
sounding invisibly in the extra-planetary air
grieving and dissatisfaction coming home
don't get sucked up into the human trap
not again and the woman hanging her tresses
out to dry and the harpist surrounded by
gold and its counterfeit like all learning hollow
each alphabet the narrow tract of incision
and interpretation adding up to zero morph
the dead alone in their lithiform silence
of inexorability ending unless it is a trap
spelling the interior of a hive or an ant-heap
dressed in skin of unabashed longing promenade
along the Ionian littoral speaking as philosophers
about the germane and the unknown and the hapless
stars up above exchanging fates with the demi-gods
who have been tricked by the lure of immortality
when it is only a shell game in a dockyard
waiting for the boat to Sicily to set sail
how many thousand years ago

the day I was the first to reach the blackboard
and conjugate the verb esse *in all its persons moods*

tenses voice number and infinitives participles gerunds
could hear singing from within the minute hand
that held the chalk of inexorability the endings
which have no inception the radii of an Egyptian sun
like intangible spokes fanning an impossibly dense air
music as if issuing from the horn of an imaginary beast
flowers iridescently blue ornamenting the hem of a goddess
futile in her beauty casting impossibilities to summer winds
as if to chastise crocus and narcissus alike the drowning
the evanescent glimmer of light in the fading eye
chalky spirals of numinous letters the instantaneous
poetry of smoke and salty wave noon at its brimming
in a trance speaking the irreducible language of fire
brow lit up by the incendiary loom of inspiration
could feel the itching in the back brain the crawling
feverish insects of madness who devour whole the cortex
leaving me woofing on all fours on a shaking plane
eating as it were the Pythagorean logarithms
that are the consummation of sand and lust
who could see or hear me? who was there?
isles of the blessed crashing into the volcano
where the oracle divides its tongue into multiples of five
and shatters all imagination with fiery prediction
thus ends the ancient world a ruin of marble and dust
vowels and diphthongs littered in wreckage of grass
hoof prints and howling in the waste mountain
where shepherds recite the abacus of lunacy
being in love with the forever goddess

inexorability of the chain letter sent from Mycenae
to the stews and dives of Piraeus in which detailed
the affairs of unbidden and now nameless
how is it the one the shape of smoke the haunting
a reckless dissent from the Theogony a swarm
blackening the sanctuary and its tripod
all eventualities confined to this one dying

confessions of an alphabet-master to his swans
on the walls graffiti tell of one-eyed loves and arms
swarthy municipal figures bought out by a crone
in the twilit fundament of the end of the story
who are blind and vicious denouncing gods
writing and rewriting the same ending
the Wheel now on the descent and its water
spilling over the sun-burnt pasture lands
at the end of the story and sent home
to the darkening western lands the agony
loss and disaccord

the Unreal Omegas

ᚠ

LABYRINTHYS
HIC . HABITAT
MINOTAVRVS

Berkeley CA, Dec. 5, 2014-Jan. 8, 2015

ALTERTUMSWISSENSCHAFT

tot quan vuelh ai quan de vos me sove
Rigaut de Berbezilh

I

the greater Bear and the lesser Bear
the belt of Orion and the Pleiades awash with light
what scintillations of the Orient reveal
that we'll never know past midlife beyond the age
when years recalled like instants passed and
nothing more remains but faint signals turning pale
I was here once among the partridge and the quail
a darting image in the bird's eye a shadow a
is there a constellation where the Sick-bed lies
a galaxy where Malady and Sickness and Depravity
light up flashing with a million malignant lights
are there other universes where the Chance to *be* again
resides and the romping passage of Brother in his small
revolve in the many distant grasses of loss and grief
can it be the Archaic World in its bas-relief of Light
is more than just the chronicles of sand and dust
the insectary where gods played out their futile games
for mortals who weary of the Promise undid themselves
did not the luminous circle called Bernice's Lock shine
amidst the starry divulgations of Fable and Delight
an unwritten poetry of beams and saucers and glass
reflected in the Dreamer's dream of being alive again
I was here once exuding breath and sweat and fastened
to the poles of flame for the brief instant of havoc and
the hammer the cleavers the screw the pinch and the bellows
sounding a device of forlorn and longing in stanzas round
and Mind startled by the creaking winch the flapping sails
arouses its unsettled thoughts and for a second bursts

through the grey and shuttered walls to plunge into the Ether
that like an ocean surrounds the world of intricacy and form
to become of them One burning to have a name and sing
to remember just for once the ring of meters and the coil
unwinding when Dawn a dewy field unveils before the Eye
and the earth of matter and shape and substance comes to be
with its cities of cyclopean walls and subterranean myths of
childhood this fleeting image like pages in a disappearing book
soldiers fully clad in brassy armor rising from the furrows
call to one another angrily the hazy clarions of legend
themselves in a trice destroy in the clangor of passing time
and just so the fullness of things becomes a hollow *ting!*
no recall of burial rites of stones that at midnight speak
of the exchange of hands and brides and brightnesses
beyond compare a rush of days in ivory and obsidian
just the marrow at the core of death the ash of Evening drear
I was here once playing charades with the many girls
chair and rug clepsydra and the tolling clock guess who
was it born among the caryatids did it flourish then
when islands walked on stilts towards petty kingdoms
whose boast was the genealogy of giants and massy rock
was it just blocks from the Hospital which is the labyrinth
and with it were there not the multiple names of the Hero
the jeopardized and often solemn tales true and untrue of
just who was born first and who came after to steal the pelt
and who quarreling threw the unaimed javelin and hit
the magic deer in passing so much riot and confusion
the color of dark ivy and smoke the uncounted persons
dazzled by the meridian's awful lamp and fell into ditches
fodder for birds of prey and dogs no more lies to tell
fragments of and anxious too when I was here the once
a section of some greater Unknown hitherto   red
Arcturus Betelgeuse Aufklärung Spectacular Diseases
in each wight in each piece of carrion some consciousness
the sundered portions falling weightless through the light
diminishing and diminished by lunacy and obsession

here was the Cloaca Maxima here was the Pantheon here
infernal side exits to the underworld by the grassy knolls
that mark the once opulent tombs of senators and knights
still hear the legions marching in great echoed whispers
down the Via Appia corollas of red dust swooning air
swaths of honey suckle and grape vine patches on the hill
a dialect almost comprehensible buzzing in the sullen brush
far sleeping the arm grown numb and useless transpiration
the brow its fevered recollection of atrium or peristyle
women in bunches pulling on an enormous loom colors
woven into the gathering dark of history's slow eclipse
listen to tanners and rabid dogs barking in the alleyways
the temptress with her goddess hairdo stepping lightly
over the marble threshold into the overheated dormer
faces thick as thumbs and twice as deaf agape with wine
strewn like noontime shadows their bodies in the triclinium
twitching with some divine reverie or oracular mistake
chronicles of the immense Afterlife recited in a blur
of voices multiple and overdubbed stammering wet
offering the mystic secret of Pythagoras to the blind
pyramids and ellipses and rotating spheres of night
all a wasteland an endless sheet of sand and porphyry
here I once stood seeking the Number and its other
sirens and harpies swooped to steal my bread and seas
vacant amphitheater choruses reduced to saliva
in and out of the empty bleachers phantoms crying out
what was the form of the Idea *what was the shape eternal?*

daze the numinous   'ware the   Mars high
Mercury son of Luna   was that the last time we met
hymn to the Sun   the all but deserted hotel lobby
the shy red head hiding behind the magazine stand
would be the one to announce your death
the world has no edges at all   a circumference
which fills the imagination with dread   seas
bottomless and that do not   all the horizon

a plenitude of nothing   tempted the ore by
stained the hands   flight is coming soon
and a man will be sustained by his own will
when I recall that we both talked simultaneously
it is no wonder that I do not remember who
the days of the week each with their planetary house
accommodated the head   for entry into
crematoria lining the route however invisible
the giants' causeway a thing of legend
you talked about the archaeology of water
      about the rumination of the stars
about the divinity that possessed you about the
dark finally and the principles upon which time rests
not for a moment but forever on the other side of Mind
with Venus in flux and the Crab and Capricorn entering
Aquarius   a white light at first faint then a
dazzling   issuing from the tomb of Cecilia Metella
what was the mystery about the bark setting forth
the day had gone its first quarter plus ten when
      sails motionless in the bright air
Misenum just off in the distance bathed in luminosity
invisible the hoof that smote your brow
what's there to understand about a shadow
      a thin plume whitish in shape
before the thunder and in the   poorly lit
below the portico where rust lies in wait   a radio
message from down under // who bit into the pomegranate
the reward of hemispheres of time a darker summer
a fission in the vowel held for its quantity and
   falling down the marble parapet seeing *"things"*
swarms of black dots consuming the   flush
at the margins words scribbled   descended
from king Lars Porsenna   at the third milestone
you continued to talk about crystals and roses even
as the evening lowered its intimidating curtain
and you could hear motor cars outside idling

and the signals of cicadas in the darkening ivy
where leaf confers with leaf   nocturnal sands
where you would sleep   finally and alone

II

AENIGMATA and the names for things that have no shape
the constant rain that inundates unmarked fields the cries
from nowhere that echo in sleep the white chalk marks
delimiting what it is a man can think when out of his mind
erasures   *when are we ever really ourselves?*
where the finite world ends the infinite world begins
what's the difference?
and we saw the pyramids which are enormous tombs
and the Sphinx that is a statue half lioness half woman
though the Persians had the best of us we suffered little
and made our way back up the Nile
seeing many exotic animals crocodiles ostriches and the like
what did we learn and what was it for?
in her grey teacher's smock walking up and down the aisle
owl-eyed Minerva she who measures goddess of a thousand works
how can we be alike? how can one be more than the other?
Joseph who derives from the sequence of votaries
sacred to the moon or from some deeper *askesis*
him speaking I follow shadow-like through Hades
is it what we are asking for that we cannot find
which is the island of the many of the many amnesia
fourfold targets on the run her Bow aimed
the deadly through thick green undergrowth
the boy parallel to the Joseph counting sand
stretched out on the great mappa mundi stargazing
him shadow-like through Hades I multiply Joseph
startled out of his ikon of pure gold plate a water
suffused his lenses darkening a foil in hand the target
a hind chasing through afternoon hills of dun
if western further to go naming trees in an alphabet

between each finger a sign that we will recognize
though we may never come back this way
still a Joseph in dreams talking with my mouth
for sure the same way it was in the grass
when the finger went lost and the sirens and the night
going in circles shadow-like though Hades
to the house dormant come the twain a hush faint
perplex of the many-sided rebus of language
which cannot be interpreted aright the many think
it is a cave deep near the grove of Nemi and its pool
that we will go together into the holy woods
what is there to fear from a book or an oracle
the Sibyl in her bottle the raving silence
when the sun at its highest and the light slants
pure as Joseph like glass reflecting ubiquitously
like something the shape of ink spreading its stain
demonstrating *the* archaic city augmented
in its own sky of fleece and ruddy cornerstones
is it that a Joseph is there *too* a fundamental shade
a perspicacity of moonbeams and mercurial
what is there about a shadow to know him
following through intricacies of Hades wedge
and lyre and bombast of hidden grottos the
ever more ancient more fleeting light through
masonry of music strung a prize for Icarus
example of fair sonants and vocables strange
Joseph is one and who then is the *other*
    AENIGMATA
the shape of words for things that do not exist

watching from afar
the restless lands the shifting littoral the attack
from nowhere of the   lifting their spears
shields reflecting Cynthia's wavering beams
and unawares the next time is here the grieving
the so many asterisks and points of no return

the restaurant where the Greeks talk blood and
wishing it would all go away was I really that boy
somewhere between winter's least punctuation
and the day the ship set sail for Messina
LA NAVE È IN PARTENZA!
gorgon and medusa things unseen for which only
sleep contains the shapes and the roiling sea
glass waves darkening at the pith and Neptune
his hoary green locks shaking in the narrow
trident aimed at the sun's eye this nightmare
we are locked in half submerged in the myth
and the marble sockets that stare into the blank
walking and walking round the obelisk of Cleopatra
sure that a pact has been signed and we are free
to wake but for what parenthetical clauses
antiquities broken off at the mid line a nausea
brimming just under the tropic of forever
could not have been that boy in winter's steel
forcing a window to frost some air to abate
running after breath circling in the forbidden
and if it is not Joseph and the Bible lessons
and the long cursive script burning in mid air
to read the words of it as they disappear in smoke
scraping chairs across the cement floor
to remember a name to have been that one
someone shouting in the plural ear of the dreamer
to come to terms with the conspiracy that
brought the Republic down and
though we may never come back this way
unrecalled vowels meters diphthongs that cling
a language at once lucid and oblique
of oblivion the steps that descend from the
considering that summer has but three months
and they are now all a ruin of circular heat
reaching out to the statue of Minerva for some
knowledge that can explain this spiraling downwards

face in the camouflage of dialect and spore
swarms of imps myrmidons wasps
and somehow improbably in the bright distance
Aetna issuing its fan of sparks and choking density
forgetting how to speak how to use hands
standing there transformed into statuary
as the lava sends its unwritten volumes down
tomorrow we will return to Siracusa
for the rites of Dionysus

AENIGMATA
(the Mystery of Silence)

what hovers after the passage
of the red planet into its obituary
the quarrels about existence and essence
and coming and becoming the Gnostics herald
and the mountain that once had wings
the power of levitation and the sorrow afterwards
from the estuary of the Nile with what boats left
returned we then our heads full of oriental marvels
and beasts such as live on the sands of sleep
and thence to Tartessos beyond the Pillars of Hercules
who will recall   the ineffable
a *sign* living in the starry delta of the heavens
signaling   signaling   what

LA NAVE È IN PARTENZA!

III

Suonavan trombe e corni e tamburini,
Come il mondo arda e tutto il cel ruini.
                    Boiardo, Orlando innamorato

the years *foam on the tide* spent in a minute's light

as if the earth to burn and bring down the sky
the disappeared the forever gone the phantoms now
legends vanished *dew on the grass* voices without shape
echo that outlasts marble frieze immemorial of air
by what trickling rivulet lay down the face and weep
gone under the many green the layers of uncounted
names whose pronunciation is no louder than a moon ray
here take this hand and feel its pulsing sinewy rhythm
grip it clasp it let it go forever into soft oblivion now
we have been there *labyrinth of time* searching for a
nothing having said the necessary in a few short syllables
endowed with dust for masks and the tenancy of breath
rented to the undersigned for these brief instants of
sounded trumpets and horns and tambourines
all manner of spectacle in the swiftly fading twilight
called out to the passing shadows *Beware the assassin!*
in darkened archways listened to the swallow's flight
like scissors silently cutting at the pattern of the clouds
aslant the sun's lamp regresses into the orangery
beyond the smallest whisper of the invading ivy
I will be there waiting wistfully you a vestal virgin
torn from a textbook illustration sixty winters ago
and number the columns parading around the Pantheon
mummers caryatids fauns satyrs Nymphs *attendants of death*
wet skin bodies young and supple and yet *darkness* the song
we are climbing without reason the vertiginous steps of ruin
a rhetoric divides us from the other world below of heat
our nostrils suffused with a dense incense musk sandalwood
we will go on sleeping like this on worn paving stones
no distinct memory to sustain us nothing but some embers
where we have been *islands of longing* is today of no consequence
the ambiguous shape of *Empire* wavers before us like a mirage
painted stones mossy tow paths derelict alleys of the Sun
round and round the millstone like blind beasts we ply
endless noon of asbestos and alabaster mourning *something*
sting of salt tears wounds never quite healed of the past

warring with ants mites chinches midges mercilessly
carving a path out of the mud of futility near Ancona
as if a next page of the directory existed as if a blade
withering in the meridian's furnace blast just off shore
where the galleys drift ghost-like knocking against dry piles
shooting for the hills on Diana's traces for a cool leaf
to stanch the fever blistered mind's *arrow swift* raving
her skirts tight around the knees a glass memory of
and in the indentations where Caesar jotted some notes
about the inhabitants of Cantium minute dots wriggling
it has all come to pass the wood-cutters the surgeons
the barbers in their blood stained smocks the pair of
mirrors held up to catch the shadow's reflection passing
intimations of poetry *trombe e corni* the rot in the pool
where Narcissus took the dive looking to kiss his own face
is literary criticism just sheer insolence and fawning envy
or are we merely working our way into the Middle Ages
a sort of Byzantine acid Sunday remote with verdigris
mosaic representations of a holy trinity on its knees
La Beffana and woofing after Diana's bare thighs and grass
icons of Mother Mercy in a run of bleeding stigmata
depictions of an afterlife in the slums of Calabria
Monica Vitti Gina Lollobrigida Anna Magnani
stations of the cross reorientations of *la dolce vita*
ides of march the closest thing to Black Monday a woe
the werewolf lurking behind the stripped petrol stations
erected in the shadow of the Coliseum , remember that?

the caves of Aeolus haunting *insecticide* of the numerous
small bricks worn at the ankle a flounce a torn upper part
the section where the planet intersected by a fluid light
and above the canopy of painted stars named after myths
Orestes fleeing from a caravanserai of ululating Furies
sky brought down a wreck to burning earth its tent
a fuselage of oil slicks and uprooted eucalypti
at the top of the hill a palace shining // mesmerism

the people who live there are dead // trance dancing
is there anyone who remembers the way back?
in the defiles of Thessaly a lone member stalking
memory's outcamp the dredges and ditches and
pornographic graffiti notched into the still burning
stakes marking each a hundred lives' distance
I was here I was here and I was here being alive
yet all around I feel a life winding down the silence
a pallor in the midst of day's bright azure hhhhhh
shifts from red to ochre the blasted heath a
certain of nothing and skin once moist to dry
a section of time marmoreal and solid dissolves
in each grain of sand the universe of galaxies
rushing like a secret wind out of the catastrophe
of air and the babble of oracular voices signs
smoking distaff chains of rust things unknown
blowing across the waste   fragmented
consciousness the unwritten page   silence
which is the greater Mystery

IV

to be "philosophical" to finish last quiescent
the small inscription on the monument of air
section by section of Gaia torn away from sleep
questioning the utilities and their homophones
a tyrannicide hiding in the sanctuary of grief
what does it say to do other than
what is the supreme number?   fled
before what had appeared to be an inferior force
through the mountain wastes and taverns
a host of cryptic glyphs menacing in formation
announce the invariable postulates of an axiom
quarrelling invective the poisonous "thought"
the stillness sitting in the midday sun alone

and with   dolorous attitude toward life
each of us come into it to suffer et cetera
wayward seas drawn by the moon into sessions
of rust and silence it is distance I mean and
caryatids blanched and eyeless upended
by cycles of heat imported by the poets
from Cyrenaica and songs of simoon and
tramontane with their haunting lyrics of sand
sophist and gnostic epicure and stoic hands
of invisibility et cetera I mean pools like eyes
in the desert profound that go all the way
to the Antipodes and the heraclitean flux and
the proposition NIHIL EX NILO GIGNI POTEST
they are athirst the errant gods of the watering hole
withered palm fronds for eyelids battered shells for ears
lie panting in the gasoline sump just outside of Hades
to make of the verb *to be* the goal of all rhetoric
hunh?   dumped the old body desiccated of its soul
next to the syllabary employed by the Ionians when
and the King of Kings on his glassy throne watching
with awe and despair the sinking of his massive fleet
abandoned by Ahuramazda and the promise of a garden
suspended above the cataracts of the Nile and the
zodiacal palaces of astrologer and sybarite burning
as is the rest of the archaic ecumene of stolen marble
come with me on a junket to the Lamp
like dusty cattle dazed and wandering transformations
of the enchantress Circe searching for their *being*
a thing of never was the massive past of space
tintinnabulating in the dusky cups of Olympus
where deities designed by absinth blinded bards
pretend the game of dice and lore   Fie!
epistemology and star-gazing the fabric rent
a tumbling sequence of worlds the size of atoms
we are all at a loss and   from the orient
mysteries arrive on knotted ropes while sleeping

a dream of reincarnation and illusive codes
Thou art That cuneiform abracadabra   ZOE
symposium   think tank   how the nameless
dispossessed of the Suburra cling to phantoms
a suggestion of beauty at the end of the dark
for whom words are puzzles of phonetic decay
a meaningless jaunt through mind a   phhhhhhhhhh
what is knowledge but a definition of
what exactly *they* mean by that   et cetera
the late emperor who lay with his sister nightly
found his severed right hand in the baths
tied to a pythagorean equation   weight of fifteen stone
hamadryads of split-brain theory naiads
dryads in Dialogue with the other just as noon
back streets where the mimes exercise the volcano
Empedocles ?   who walked into living flame
and the myriad circles that separate cause and effect
dreams with the names of planets widening
the distance between solitude and death
Ares in conjunction with Pluto the far flung
is it music that derives from the southern hemisphere
the hypotenuse in full swing above the dewfall
sounds of a celestial sublimity beyond
what any mountain can recall   *hastening*
into the Agora one day I chanced on Alkibiades
and talked we then of the trial of Sokrates
what fell light spent its luster on false etymologies?
and four hundred years later Catilina conspiring
and the death rattle of the Republic young blades
for want of money and Cicero how long abuse
his patience et cetera   grammar of unreason
pleading at the bar for some electricity
for some clear way out of the dilemma
that of the soul and its unembroidered cloth
temet nosce   beginning to forget
everything I ever learned   turn signals

how come we to this crossroads and whence
each lesson so carefully understood awash
blanks and random incisions in memory
the boy I used to be at the end of the street
where the large empty villa stands a ruin
trying to read the graffiti   haunting
chalk traces warning about the rains
and Parmenides the world of appearances
you *cannot* go back   the unchanging real
forgetting all there was to remember
ritual and bloom and desire and
the obfuscation of sleep turned inwards softly
clouds and the abrupt end of time
from whose limit the body falls leaving no trace
smoke illusions shadow coils hastening vowels
by degrees the planet curves out of control
chaos   xnhctysnkklm
(sequitur serpes fallax   diabolus
shapes the size of ink talk talking nightly
through widths of mania a divinity
scours
                    Cadmus
who devised letters from the flight of birds
and come to earth and preached with stones
hjnbshhhhh
)   luna artifex
pulcherrima   born to be wild

                    γνῶθι σεαυτόν

                    V

cloud twelve the fragment , angel face , as if blowing ,
smoke from beyond , or the real smoke which , the
event requires , wearing just a shimmy , a thrown die ,
looming , a mask , cothurns , the jimmied safe door ,

operation Orestes , furious and avenging , top-heavy
and still balanced , on stage , fuming disregard for ,
which can be considered , celestial , which merely
ecumenical , worlds floating near and far , peaks ,
cloud eight section , speaking an attic dialect , trumped
and screwed , Venus of course , foam born drifting ,
from seashell to seashell , listening for , deviating from ,
anvil and bellows , the living flame , the whole air ,
on a jewel the size of heaven , it says FRATER MEUS
, cataracts , enormous flares , jungles of silver ammonium ,
pyramids juxtaposed occupy , the hemispheres , every
form of duality , seizures and catapults , talking only ,
from the right side , oral habits of grace , integers
mounting , to the highest form of N , eyes like tigers ,
incisions just below the belt , of Orion , horizons
so infinite only an inch , will fit , transitory grasses ,
lost fingers , evenings in the delta of F , swooning like
, the Apokropolis! , statuary resembling nothing , flesh
and fish , bird-like women with harmonic , convergence ,
red hair , the sequence of others , masked , duplicates
of gods , who remain nameless , who bear earths beneath ,
their nails , who eat cancer nightly , announced the , dying ,
continents just below Egypt , classical formations , repeated
syllogisms of ink , color of inhalations , of figure 8's , who
walks on ether , sizing up the whole , the Whole , that is ,
naked being , pink action , sand which is ontology , sand
which is articulation , definite and indefinite moons , tide ,
rip , ripping , friction , edifices uncontrollably , white and ,
margins replete with ampersands , rivers of drowned , the ,
entire hesperian zone , ablaze! , Zeus in a muddy toga, Hera
's white shoulders , singed by the abacus of , grammatology ,
madness , capsules of betagrams , alpha heroin delirium ,
zed reconstructed by light , thunder in the ear of , Dionysus ,
who reappears in dreams , zodiacal and cunning , fraternal
evanescence , brief interludes , drunken jazzphone , elephants
imported from Tuscany , that fill mirrors , that stalk green ,

that destroy , rampant ivy , climbing summers , long , a ,
smaller than , remembered the , Mausoleum of Asia ,
Minor , consortium of mapologists , hovering UFOs ,
paranoia running the highway , *"they're coming!"* , hunh? ,
the dread Eumenides , miasma of the Atreids , decibels
of doom drumming , equator inverted , galactic mummy ,
speaking *zzzs* , asleep , forever , Adelphia! cloud thirteen ,
invention of time , soliloquy of water , archaeology of Mu ,
hispid creatures , wet , serpentine , syllable of no return ,
Boetia and Arcadia , lingual consonants , phonemic destruction ,
secret love , indigo shifts , porches governed by insects ,
circularity of heat , the month that ceased , to exist , dark-
ness , exclamation marks! bee swarms of Hybla , beauty ,
MORTUUS EST ,
power of omega , only once , dilapidated and pharaonic Eye ,
from Knossos to the , Park , circling and circling , roar of
terror , beasts crowded into smoke , what goes backwards ,
what sleepwalks the stairs , what is the self , but the other ,
what is the tongue , red-eyed brimming with , odor of blood
, dense choking , swift , and sweat and nausea , end of a ,
life , of a life , end of time in a , traveled this road , before ,
Circe , Calypso , Nausicaa , known them all , tremendous
drill in the , brain , litters of ants , applause , blank , s ,
ab urbe condita (AUC) , shadows of substance , eyeless
photon reverie , outside the Pantheon , one in the morning ,
look-alikes of emperor Caligula , rutting , exhalations of
rho , when empire and hovel , //////// , energies totemized ,
recycled to planet X , amazing disturbance of death , cloud
nineteen hundred thirty nine , a lawn , some rectangles of ,
on their knees , the little twosome , one of them is me ,
the other one is also me, calculating the year from the ,
Janus double-browed , brassy knell , painted on the outside
, to resemble , omicron and pi quarreling , transferred the
lares , and penates , ninth grade vestal virgin , blown candle ,
oxymoron , snowing in five minutes , memorials lain to ,
ashes scattered over mount Pindus , chorus of , hhhhhhhhhhhhh

truth is , never was , agony of lambda , fusion of epsilon ,
never expected to   ,
just a , whisper

AVE ATQUE VALE

VI

GLADIATORI MEO AMORE
Φύσις /natura of which I am a part
and proceeding as does poetry from the whole
singing innate the *κόσμος* or *Habitaculum Dei*
fragments as we are on this wandering gyre
somewhere between the Plutonian realm
and as does poetry issuing from the unconscious
but not the unfelt and into the starry kingdom
and the upper reaches of the ether belt and beyond
it's your birthday too *ποίησις* "reconciles thought
with matter and time" what we make of it
extracting from the entirety the multiplicity
of parts I am that too insubstantial snaking
and weaving through dark exploits of space
never far from the *you* which is the other half
the part that makes the whole a difficulty
to comprehend a brightness of the moment
of coming to light not asunder but everything
at once and subcutaneous and galactic and
measured by the sands that exist as a song
counting backwards from the invention of the lyre
tortoise shell and gut-string and today as
on no other the empyrean is within *me* and
I devolve in a remote pythagorean theorem
music of the spheres lunar house thirteen
winter afternoon when darkness is the *all*
being born in the repeated numeral of heat
not beside you but *as* you! quintessence and

suburb of bone and script rewriting the *code*
end all of *being* which it is on the margins
of the knowable
does the body come back again and if so
in what form and in what province of empire?
I thought to have seen some aspect of it
walking the rocky stubble of Caria
flute in hand Phyrgian cap aslant on head
was it the physical body or an umbratile figment?
can we reinvent a life just lost? the *same* life?
marigold crocus hyacinth jasmine narcissus
observable phenomena imperceptibly perishing
how is it we see through the shimmering sublime
and just as quickly fall from the world
of shining and color into the atavistic swamp
clarion call of distant birds making letters fly
to read aright the celestial graph just *once*!
dreams the shape and size of ink spreading
across the suddenly conceived *Idea* of time
rock formations battlements cyclopean walls
and the life invented moving in and out
of its self contained labyrinth mapping
its reincarnated past anew recalling fresh
the morning dewfall the sparklers the *air*!
moving slowly across the Minoan realm
lion and panther melding into dun colored stone
from afar cries of wilderness the swinging leaf
the smallest grass ants of two-fold nature &
Psyche in her paper personality about to
become invisible and the Beast and rounding
the waters infernal the Boatman who waits
who waits and waits the darkening hours
for the body physical to arrive and hoist
a stuttering hand and make the gyres shake
everything that comes around in *Physis*
and breaks apart the many integers ah!

---

to reconstruct that life *Ζωη*
reframed a pallid haunting comes unawares
up the back stairs and into the mausoleum
on the right of the baths plunging mysteriously
into the depths who hears the cry?
elfin twists of fate lesser caryatids dwindling
in the marble shadow of Ionian conjecture
a capsized soul barely afloat in the great pool
bereft of body of sense of orientation
was the sun ever so high so far so mighty
then come the snows five years and the path
obliterated that led to the Oracle and the
you know what it was the archaic thing
half-hidden in the gateway holding a mask
who will it be?
gymnosophists caught in the maze of dust
questioning the *this* and the *that* memorizing
hieratic odes two thousand years in the making
without understanding the purport of the sounds
carefully inserting into the massive phonology
a tonality of breath and rhythm amazing *techne*
unparalleled beauty of the Unheard Note
et cetera you've heard all that before the
stuff about transmigration of souls metempsychosis
and karma and the reduct of nothingness
what lies beyond the Eleusinian Fields
and the business of Persephone and Demeter
measuring strictly the time to sow and the time to die
half a year here half a year there and the pomegranate
the dire red seed the height of day and its longing
swimming in the after waters with Narcissus
gone lost like Hylas who has become an echo
mourned by Herakles as you are a half of air
a brief memory of grass in the evening fade
hard by the temple of Poseidon

VII

FLAMMANTIA MOENIA MUNDI
in the late morning of my life   already
noon an impossibility // swelling darkness
f   lood   moon   s
m   ourning   a life'   s long
the welkin pouring   through   like
tear   s   pitched from the boat   !
d   azzled by (the) l   ight
inf   ormed   shape les   sly
h   ound   s   re   deyed   D   iana
sen t   m   ortal s to   fla y
a   son g of   s kin a   h   igh
v   oice   l   eaf   r   ent
b   leed s   m yth   e cho es
)   so it goes origins and origins   plied
on the watery   loom   finger s dight a pl   ay
words made up of flight!   sh ifts   red   of
scan   s oval in height   a mpersand   s
forge   d in   a i   r   y round   s
tri   de nt   part   s depth   s
ZEUS   & MAMMON   and the beast   s
that ROARRRRRRRRRRRR
forms are real only in dreams   (
when the sounds of things vanish
what swills then deepening the loss its threnody
a bright once was summer's errant hour
gone a man's too shadow in form like
unto him long passed below the Hellespont
his watery bier was // that was in weight and
substantially in appearance like a god and
waved from many a distance to the Wain in passing
goddesses and lesser sprites shining whose
was that name whose the sequence of beings
at the altar placed the human sacrifice to appease

what stomping hill dialect speaking Deity
& reappear in altered states the mind its play
drugged on hemp and hemlock the image
sailing through glassy straits to Panormus
sparkling on its hills beneath the imminent starry
were wars declared and armies marching up and down
deriding hummock and dale alike the tread
a man's a wheel in constant flux
'til one day the Arrow cuts through the spokes
did it make sense that rutting in the pines
running amok the youthful ephebes of Lacedemon
sparring their naked muscularity a Bong!
atoms irreducible in theory in swarms invisible
shape the very thought of it , you know?
here Sokrates tread the stony path of quest
and Perikles orated empire thalassocracy
acanthus and corinthian stele spotless in the sun
a vast the rounding water of history thousands
what is number anyway in the passing of soul to soul
migrants like myrmidons in insubstantial ether
"flaming ramparts of the universe"
trading wings like angels stoned on Love
thithering in the endless yawn of time
to erase and remake Persepolis and imitate the Light
waking on the sandy heights of orient
to question and be questioned by the gods of Hindustan
revolve the thread and spire and Perish , Dear One
inside out the womb our day is done
down the second street our shadows walking still
do chatter on about the time
when a man could walk a kingdom in a day
our shadows our morning our final transit
does it matter how many dialects we mastered
how many puzzling tomes we devoured
what was the moment of highest inspiration
if not the night lost drinking in the Tavern

VIII

a dark forest what does that mean
one clings to Beauty and otherwhere Beauty
ceases to exist and we take from the quarry
what we find and of it build a temple
coming from the bleak glade into some light
a conjecture of time a mass of space
between what is loved and what cannot
abbreviate the days of a life a question
plagues the errant mind as always plucking
from the dangling branch a voice to use
and sing Yea the forms and shapes of Beauty
defining what is drilled in the shell and
taking from salt water the Image to shine
as if in a dream moving slowly through the grove
the darkening which is an afterthought of
what cannot be recalled with clarity a summer
noon a session with the sophists in the portico
gathering dust and humus and making of it
what the oracle demanded a secret cleft
as if to listen in off moments for the echo
surely a deity will be speaking hoarsely
to the unbidden ear and spread out in the brain
the map of the heavens as a type of mind
and looking around dazed hearing the scamper
shuffle of fallen leaves in the remote and evening
again the unclear and where She stood
surrounded by her wood nymphs and a water
sounding in the otherness who will contradict
that this is a vision a shimmering of air
conceits of hair in bunches and the madness
of her mouth erratic and red promising what
laden with earthly riddles go then into

the labyrinth of Eros deciding nothing of the
present shaping with unsure hands the atmosphere
whence Beauty derives her goodness and
not waking ever but in that sleep of the Hour
shifting through the accolades of red
into the murmuring Bay just feet away
a music of perhaps and never again a chord
struck between the tangled twigs overhead
here sit a while and compose the lyric braid
twining it through vowels of incomplete sand
let nothing sway the silent decibels that move
as shadows of remembrances however vague
a world is gone just like that by sifting
through the immobile grasses beside the Pool
neither finger nor rusted blade appear
and for a long afternoon remain there haunted
by the indistinct recollection of Beauty
bathed in her skin of lunar transparency
summoning with her slightest nod Diana
to avenge whatever corrupt syllables occur
stuttering grammar that offends the Light
a stinging shaft may fly from her taut bow
fixing the heart with some measure of intellect
by which to know how tides do rise and fall
some hue of knowledge extracted from dew
a pigmentation that colors the unknown sky
as it rises over the dim Ionian distances
shedding a brief luster on the vanishing page
the vanishing page

IX
ET EGO IN ARCADIA

nostalgia for the never been the islands green of
how does it go away what is scarce recalled
numbness of the sleeping finger the missing call

afflicted by the Muse sent to the sanitarium
near Mount Parnassus to reconstruct ivy
the climbing sensation of heavens within
go away then section by section the office of time
the quotations and paragraphs left blank
Daphne raving at the root the sacred touch
pearled essences of dew the brow encumber
as dazed the wandering soul lonely quests
through Arcadia's dim phantom presence
were there lacustrine cities here a longing
for otherness a glade creeping darkly waters
that returned no reflections moons finite
in number crowning the soft Etruscan hills
yet it does go away the furrowed sleep of time
head down in the mythiform cavity of Momus
listening from afar the recitations of tragedians
vowels of intermediate sand accents heightened
to the excess of red and then disappearance
one after another of the remembered *personae*
slipping imperceptibly from view the echo
not once or twice but who knows the horizon
beyond which the other world either begins
or ends hues of dappled and dun evanescence
wall paintings of the legend of Fade and Pale
goat footed others dancing to the foreign pipe
like the time you and I approaching the dream
from the other side suffered transformation
each becoming what the other least suspected
and in the ravines a deity started whooping
and in the sky vehicles powder blue passed
like clouds on the missing summer day
the news was the passage of poetry bright and
multiply voiced coming from nowhere trees
and rocks and rivulets in a chorus of cryptic
or like the other time when we missed the movie
spent hours beneath the bridge skipping stones

was it Zeus disguised as a horned ram that
bade us surrender to the Unapproachable?
I feel bogged down sluggish mired hopeless
these once verdant meadows these hillocks
groves of ilex and birch plots of eglantine &
where shrilled the shepherd's reed and great Pan
scampered over rocky clefts singing long the heat
circling in ever greater gyres and the day of months
extending down to the river bank where Naiads
precious and few washed their unbraided locks
and seeing us puzzled an insect grazed their eyes
how came we hence in hand the book of Thought
unreason snapped its violent chord we danced
cutting our bare feet on fierce nettle beds
we watched as swarms flying swiftly from the Box
darkened the once glass pure meridian air
this day not of celebration but of emptiness
it will be tomorrow ere the noon's clock is up
the ear dulls with intonation of the Untranslatable
were we to look again at one another the scales
of recognition will have fallen and dust deposits
in burning heaps ashes flying in a desert wind
our hopes and names and playful masks rent
and news of great Pan's unexpected death!
immense languishing grayness and the dull phone
that resounds pointlessly in the sodden grave
no more recall the mornings in the flying sea
sheen and bottle green the joyful waves above
the remote skiffs with sails blown out the gulls
swooping to pluck the illusory marine lair
identities shimmering mirages floating cliffs
on high the cyclopean citadel the run of bees
making alphabets of honey in the promised light
dry mouthed bleary eyed stewed in the brain I
Chloris Phyllis and *Amaryllis* their tresses
drowned in the foggy drear how mourn they

the absent the missing the never to be again
through vale and stony path their plaint drags
see no more the shapely forms of Love but step
in intellect's distant and repeated mistake
hovering in the fantastic evening bruise
a single planet named after ruddy Ares
broods then descends disappearing behind
and Vulcan Bangs! his anvil and anger suits
the formerly sweet demesne with bristling rods
where to find hospice in this misnamed bog
or to ever pine in the blasted and weary heath
unpromised stars shuddering send their thieves
to loot the granary where Demeter keeps her swoon
bolts amiss shatter across the paper orange sky
and indigo browed Cerberus barks thrice
at Hade's balefully wide open entrance way
I know no road I have no form I am no wight
buoyed by nothing the soul levitates above sleep
the gravid seemingness of loss and depth
do you start, *Frater*? the keys no longer fit
emptied the theater sits humming with ghosts
like the last time we met and the City rocked
on a slender thread called *illumination* yes
'twas the olde Arcadia the land of dishabille
the thousand and seventy seven gods of grass
and stone harping like cicadas in the furnace
what language did they bid us use in dialogue
the firmament which all around raised its canopy
glittering with the untold and nameless planets
each a story in itself each extinct no sooner seen
away we went departures of another kind AOI
a flame of endless luster swift between my ears
traffic horns and moving hills up and down
the glistening noiseless cars sped and disappeared
a hand a leaf a gleaming glass a sudden what

this is *that* and I am in the ancient *otherwhere*

X

Mnemosyne! nothing is familiar to me any more
not the dirty snow shoring the caryatids nor
the fallen marble by the gas station what used
to be the enormous painted statue of Athena
don't recognize the road the ox-carts the way-
farers in their broad brimmed hats the straw
lining the ditches the corpses tossed to rot
what battle or war it was what proclamations
on the assembly rostrum the suspicion of weather
what year of indictment and judgment what idiolect
notched on the outer walls the broken wains
useless wheels still spinning in the dust nothing
of this at all familiar recognize no one passing
potters bakers and smithies all grime faced
winter like a cloud blanket hanging over the
nothing of this comes back to me threatening
rumbles in the air knives gleaming in alleys
puddles and pot-holes knee deep in mire
turning and returning to the same *absence*
a stool in the back of the tavern a darkness
wrapped around the muffled voices unfamiliar
indistinct powder shifts in phonetic peculiarity
ear filled with confetti nothing passes through
a new dialect gravel antinomy phosphorous
something glowing that didn't used to be a
section of time the size of Asia Minor drifting
blindly against the main where no advance exists
wherever I turn cliffs lift their oblique case
grammar falls away meaning has no sense
only unfamiliar rows of apex and decline // the
unbuttressed syntax of void and anticlimax
mouths flitting in the dark practice their hoods

reoriented syllables exit unarmed from dreams
that occur in the western lobby of the furnace
ARMITE ALCESTEI PELE THETHIS CALAINA
step out of their wrought Etruscan mirrors
shaking incense from their centuries' old hair
me they look through as if I were PRUMATHE
unbound from the rock of historical evidence
RATH with laurel branch wavering disappears
suchness and tautology chronicle an inky tale
all flows backwards where I have never stepped
does the inch filed in the pool of Nemi come back
the never once of archaic sound suddenly !!!
Mnemosyne! -s ha limb sh- kes
remember nothing of this hell-hole these diesels
traversing hour after hour the self same tract
apa and *ati* long dead how they shimmer in the
after a day at the clinic pronouncing consonants
for therapy clustered ivy darkness fell
epigraphy of sand dense nominatives call
a myth about the letter Mu a mystery a math
buried in oblivion the left eyelid flutters a sign
something else is coming some great Shadow
they will take the son of ALTHAIA from her toilet
spur him on to the boar hunt thrill him
such is death so they say from the echo chamber
glass cracked by light celestial portions obscured
breath that comes halting from the trunks
each leaf is a separate soul! crying
unknown among the unknown I recite the poem
and at the end when the similes fail to hold
the western sea comes rushing to take my hands
+++
inscribed on the scarab mirror the name URPHE
I am in his head and bring to the eye a thought
if only I could write to repossess the loss of
something else is troubling me a

oracular distances   many the swift
when they lay me down on the rocky beach
and grayness overtook the light the failing day
to kiss me a wraith in leopard skin and hair
the size of the mouth of the Nile
to kiss me wet and cold the remote a voice
never woke me
participial forms to set up a place
the figure of a mature bearded man
leaning on a gnarled stick
similar to that of RATHMTR
labeled on a mirror
represented seated in the Underworld
in the tomb of Orcus
(TINA who hurls thunderbolts)
exit *Mnemosyne*

XI

ARCANA MUNDI

the slip-knot through which the *face* appears
the static of grammar monumental errors shifting
from oracle to oracle an indigo base a device
in which the mouth fits and summons sleep
from the pedestal of the winged mountain of dreams
the one that is situated near Stabia where the mummers
all fluted in their amaranth toss-ups and stoned
appear at break of day to put an end to stealth
robbers of iniquity and troth and what makes no sense
hard by the dwelling place of dead goddesses
running underground the rushing water of oblivion
and the trees planted strategically to resemble
nothing so much as the judgment of Paris
moments of eternal stillness windless but violent air
each leaf poised as if to utter fierce denials

the Library prone and as if hushed by knives
its marble eloquence striated by afternoon blood
it is not here that I am not here a life winds down
a lack of remembrances a fault line of otherness
a career in breath a notion to write Poetry
that will remain forever illegible in its format

what is it that is up above that stutters like a hand
with no direction that elicits from the bottom of
anything the numbing the dizziness the whelmed
sense of non continuity that it happened once
but will never be remembered the same way
stepping stones that make cautiously the way
from the isle of Rhodes to the isle of Lemnos
or marmoreal quotations about the other hand's
inability to carve correctly the hieroglyphs
profusely littered in sand and made to resemble
the fallen of mind those who praying to gods
without name and section by section the canopy
of the immense and stellar fades dimming ever slowly
the branches of light or the sea underneath
where alphabets extinguished sphinxes erased
the never been of historiography outlining
but not illuminating the many assassinations
of tyrants the regicides the immolations the sacri-
fices –fices –fices pitch burning odor of resin
pines turned into skiffs water boiling margins
steaming littorals cannot see to recall the hills
sheared at the top by searing bolts of envy
and caked in white powder shoulders aquiver
HERA stands aloft the thing way up above
the enigma of her expression the misunderstanding
the absolute in its parentheses of white hot magma
stepping into the volcano reciting lyric fragments
pigmentation and code of the Mysteries

nebulous etymologies about the Origins of smoke
something flying through crystal a shot of red
leaving its infernal trace in the mind
capsized letters rho and tau
sigma hissing on the verge of thought
sudden meadows with shadow and ornament
stepping gracefully between shimmers Aphrodite
a fragrance of sandalwood and myrrh
her sea-small foot hesitant and grass
immutable and innumerable where voices
of all the lost lines of early epic murmur
aching to be heard to be revived and understood
moon stilts humming of invisible swarms
chastened brow buried in Parian marble
what else can make this poem?

in the second instance there was the warning
sirens echoing freesong above darkening waves
the edge of water seasilt tumbling sand frills
wettened the tip of the divine finger to create
between man and man enmity strife bloodshed
these colonnades acanthus-topped bluing in
the gathering dusk a mountain emergent a
flame circling faintly above the crescent sky
some hint however pale a hue of conscience
a field stained deep spreading across

ancient rock stubble as far as the eye ,
sit you here , breathe deep the night ,
a tolling of distances , dogs bark , shh ,
soon when sleep's soft engine , you ,
there , what , darker still the vast ,
takes you from the small portico ,
imagine another planet , crickets ,
weed tufts , sparse as memory ,
waning ,

who else is , there , breathing ,
dust worlds disintegrating , souls
suspended in thought , migrating ,
pale , something ringing , remote ,
a hand , at first great and shadowy ,
beside you , surrounding , lightless ,
gone

ARCANA MUNDI

XII

fuming disregard of the thirty three deities
who govern the lintel and the door frame
for the entrances and exits of those whose
shadows have been spared the passage of blood
enigmatic presences crouching on rock and heath
far from the illusive world painted on the shifting
walls of the House of Mysteries , you know ,
where we spent the last few lifetimes elusive
half blind knocking against misplaced furniture
attaching names willy nilly to the guests
whose riotous existences puzzled us over much ,
fauns and satyrs Nymphs with gorgeous red hair
naiads dripping wet from an eternity in the Pool
hamadryads sphinxes women multiply named Helen
or Selene pugilists and gladiators furious
chasing the dead through cinecittà *on rickety bicycles*
what was the sign by which we recognized *them*
coruscations iridescent in the otherwise invisible ,
tracks of the unknown the once vermillion hispid
thing at the bottom of the missing page echoes
of ampersand at war with circumflex the dialect
rotund and unrecorded spoken at hilltop speeds
whatever whispered among cities of leaf and ant
whatever dialogued between incandescence and heat
each and every found a score in the Minoan vocabulary

the alabaster white of *her* forgotten features shining
dimly in the rhetorician's recycled attic vowels
taught to pronounce without speaking//ephemeral silence
of the antipodes somewhere to the left and south of Thebes
incisions in a grain of sand the utter sadness of thought,
it's enough to cry
I feel the weight of his death throughout the building
it's not as if we didn't know the way to Epidaurus
that a man's voice could sound so sweet ,
what was the escape route , the escape route
from the excavations at Delphi to the overtones of deep
dyed carmine near Siracusa and the things underneath
and the sense of hands interpolating lost words
an air of miasma and haunting secret cries muffled
in the ditch or within the pillow where Klytemnestra slept
not what music could do or summon or revive
the cymbals the sistra the small Egyptian tom-toms
the plangent pan's pipe of the backlands the whistle
however faint of the shepherd murdered for *knowing*
what was to account for the gymnast wandering
during unlit hours from tavern to tavern
weeping in his arms the loss of Alkibiades
so much and more , the specter of sudden death
the inexplicable disappearance of so many in the pass
edges to matter darkening steeply in the dream
the last few lives we passed through the bean field
and from afar gazed at the unending construction
of the Parthenon and listened to verses of the island bards
who had *seen* with the eyes of inspiration Achilles
even as he descended from the mortal gyre
into the house of Pluto , so much and even more
looking at each other turning to stone black surfaces
remains of interstellar empires and the smoking
among the reeds a mournful voice lifting
paired flutes whose melody weaves through the walls
can come back no more , stop , cannot

and the enormous canopy of stars moving shifting
ever so slowly from the point where dawn enters
and day's futile promise of everlasting light!

XIII

read the ancient poets
study rhythm and harmony
learn to be measured and graceful
in both speech and deed
in public as well as private
I lived Loud and I loved you Best
all the rest is air and endlessness
the white and black beans
are the days and nights of man
the blue pebbles are the sea
and the green ones the mainland
count them as you would in a dream
count the passing stars of time
who live unbalanced on the tightrope
of ambition and illusion then plunge
forthright into the boundless ditch
minds blank and blind as stone
days of man fusion asbestos
yet the gods with hands and feet alike
in their Olympian mansions dustless
uncaring enjoy fruits and wine
the livelong day of immortality
making envy and ire to enter into
the hearts of heedless mortals
farseeing they are not//unmindful
of the lessons learned the poets read
the harmonies and melodies rehearsed
and dive recklessly into gambling
strife and womanizing arguing
who is the best and why and what not

free with their fists blood shed
rolling on the ground bone broken
skin the color of grape-peel
eyes the shape of night circling
the ravaged moon hair piled high
like the hives of Mount Hybla
haunting haunted hissing
her unwinding braid rounds
distant Saturn's farthest rings
deep sinks the deadly quim
her song the delta of nightmares
Kirke beast goddess of lust
temples built to the god of Ruin
earth-shaker azure doom portent
rimmed crevices a universe in length
rains of sulfur and mercury
seething attributes of meter and rhyme
to make assonance and gold
sublime in the false equation
that combines instability with death
who first of the immortals
went under struggling with fate
who questioning submitted skin
hair eyes the intricacy of echo
to the Nymph in her coral bed
ruse of lexicographers and smiths
brassy sheen of her distance
turning verdigris by night
metonymy synecdoche flagrant
delusions of language sitting tranced
at the schoolmaster's feet trying
to recall the why and when of
doubt the relapse of memory
into cycles of red and accidence
lawns of Asia Minor gazelles
palaces of mirage and sunburn

fabled kings bathed in liquid ore
shaking their ochre tridents

almighty Ahuramazda!

phases of lunar indecision
before total collapse of hills
suburban sophists buried under
miles of dust opprobrium before
chance pronouns and neuter gender
coming home before dawn
hauling the battered skiff
up on the unknown littoral
hearing in the ear of remembrance
the shuttle of the loom
going up and down ad infinitum
the dog's once familiar bark fade
so I turns to him and says
Joe, the way Neptune was looking
this morning not sage not good
hoary barnacled and half deaf
with the roaring Tyrrhenian sea
in his ear and shouting out of his
sleep about the damned gout
and the wine casks and butts
scattered over the dark floor
a god he was once a ruddy
intransigent moody deity
could have brought down
the celestial roof with a beat
all hoof and horn and bleating
out of his fumous conch shell
and Joe turns to me and cries
weeping all over the algae
and peat moss and dunes
all wet and pale shading
deep into the sea's vast wreck
once a then what nothing

arcades shattered columns
caryatids albescent and eyeless
stranded on the opposite shore
simmers sun's griddle on sands
where history has become beached
dense and noose the rhetoric
and music in Doric mode hasps
stillness a hunch hashed dying
chords snapped mind's oval disk
circling the mounds of heat
just south of the venereal port
where is no place a list of women
cataloged ship by ship their own
qualities like combs and paraffin
slatted into the unmoored wave
Altertumswissenschaft preterit
and sigmatic aorist conjugations
duplicated perfect root forms a
sense of ancient smoking water
shifts in sleep's immense ink
toward the ever disappearing
poetry recited by smaller voices
still a thread running faintly
red a lapse a tomb a silence

XIV
PHILOLOGIA (*a reconstruction*)

language taken apart section by section
until all that's left is some white unrecognizable
excavation and conjecture cannot fill the great lacunae
reconstructing small footed Myth in her green absence
taxonomy and peerage of the distant gods
whose names reside in decomposed dust and ashes
no retribution for their fictive speech acts
that created maintained then destroyed the cosmos

lapsus memoriae unrecorded integers after the BIG BANG
flaming ramparts of the universe coded in volatile lexica
hapax legomenon a blind finger tracing suggested
shapes of characters in worn stone and sand rumors
while small groups of the *learned* theorize phonetic decay
symposia on consonant clusters and circumflex disarray
accent marks diacritics distinctions of long and short
genealogies and sound shifts of prehistoric tongues
memorization of ritualized but unwritten texts
whole centuries of wandering in the steppes
communicating with unrelated tribes warring
fucking borrowing sounds imitating retroflex clicks
assigning gender changes to abstract nouns
that have nothing to do with sex or regeneration
sepia tinted recollections of the rise of dynasties
who guarded holy syllables in hypnotic mantras
to make power the shape of ink that erases formulae
and interminable days learning to record accounts
numbering amphorae vats and barrels bulk units of items
not ideas notched with slanted marks and crude ideograms
how much of anything and the value of a human life
hybris and nemesis pride defeat and downfall
all that is vaguely recalled reinvented and named history
soon it is Diana and Apollo behind etymologies of thought
cycles of events that keep being repeated and inverted
men transformed into beasts agonies of legend
pelts left out to dry skins that sing hair immensely dark
enormous sun and moon letters to account for dying
hills of dialects overlaid on each other the babble
emerging at dawn in the circumscribed temenos
and from the many one given by the Muse to poets
those maddened existing outside the loom of language
suffering auditory hallucinations lyric fragments
like shards that litter the temple pits with forgotten letters
no matter what you think they seem to be Egyptians
using the speech of statues to confirm by the flight of birds

the origins of the alphabet and the ensuing disorder
shibboleth and syncretism of textual abracadabra
dialogues with divinities who mushroom into daylight
saying this that and the other about the Origins
stone abruptly lipped against a cliff of wavering illusion
masked dancers tripping drugged on aphrodisiacs
meant to send the Mind into the future next stage
somewhere east of Lydia where fifty-breasted Artemis
harangues shaggy warrior kings with epic diphthongs
scattering monarchic sperm across the face of Chronos
in the undocumented plethora of mismatched syllables
to encounter one complete line of dactylic hexameter
describing the woe and burning of queen Dido!
imperfections misinterpretations glosses echolalia
schoolboys made to sit on hard benches learning by rote
to enumerate quantities of meter and verb formations
in the puzzling afternoon light descending from a sun
that went missing eons before the calculations of Ptolemy
assonant gold envy withering indigo noon mercurial heat
circularity of vowels lost in archaic Punic winds
by the banks of a former river lush vegetation & tales
desiccation of empires reduced to a thumbnail
lunar thirteen times and the riddle of the labyrinth
rock weddings storms brewing in a potion HUNH!
what remains but a metronome still ticking
in the ear of the sleeping god Dionysus
……………………………..
(*will we ever know what the original was*)

XV

the houses barely visible on the opposite shore
who dwell there suffer glossolalia and aphasia
have no memory of crossing the murky stream
assume identities of distance and smoke returning
to inhabit bodies of mountain nymphs or bees

didn't know I'd meet you again in this way
statute to statue eyeless in marble perimeters
in this deserted field buzzing with meridian heat
all yellow and high stifling the hour before the storm
the thin shiver that runs like electricity through stone

ghosts of the names of myths barely make out
shapes of certain vowels crescent and circumflex
accented on the hiatus that separates honey from air
the color of *her* eyes density of hair caught in the comb
ivory carved echoes of the hills where memory died

tired we became of the former life the dun and dusk
floating like a fog over some invisible water
remember how you cried out when night descended
with its mysteriously throbbing *caesars* and *antonios*
death was in the twitch of every distant star

meraviglia! soothsayers with sable eyes cast about
in the sand for an answer what lies beyond the houses
and if the mountain is still there beside the moon
pale refulgence of letters embroidered in the vatic wind
suchness of the *other* puzzled before the mutilation

tragedy unravels its five acts on parapets of black stone
Klytemnestra woven into a dyed cloth raves like gamma
caught in delta's liquid snare and Kassandra stung
by the mystic wasp revolves imperceptibly in a jar
we watch without understanding and turn into rooks

ages spent in the tomb of Cecilia Metella with a music
kithara sistrum bells a voice like burning indigo
haunting and ravings within walls of archaic rain
from the Hellespont to the Pillars of Herakles the world
as we will never know it again dissolves in bitter aconite

without a struggle province after province of time
falls away perishing in steppe colored weeds
we were not meant to be saved aging voicelessly
nor do signs appear in the heavens nor thunders roll
from the shattered domiciles of Zeus nor a lamp

blind hands placed on desiccated panther pelts
a rhombus or a helix involving the cicatrix of air
describe for the deaf the intricacies of phonetic decay
grand flashes of poetry riddle the maze of sandstone
through which we work like ants belittled and insane

the river that runs through it the chasm profoundly dark
the crashing of houses into the brink all night long
the transformation of language into integers of light
no more define by speech acts the *thine* and *mine*
no more embrace the sightless caryatids with bright

if there is a next life it will be the ivy on Daphne's brow
darkening that makes the brain's enigma white by turns
Apollo god of arts will be aloft denying your ancient presence
me I will no more exist than the mind before its birth
Narcissus and Hyacinth shaded red will dive into the Pool

so few the days remaining lesser yet the returning sound
remembrances of Anabasis the unending oriental pearl
suffused with dusty syallables and legendary psi and chi
thirteen moon lunacy the shifting other shore of time
oblivion lethal infusions of beauty's antidote the gone

it was sublime but was it real the unveiled Mnemosyne
greens aquiver like a rush of new spring lawns to embrace
here was the Eurotas unwinding and here Menander's bed
and just behind the Tuscan mound lies dark Nemi's lake
hithering go the nymphs that follow Echo's fatal din

yesterday was tomorrow with a shine swift fading now
oracular hum in the bedded ear of the one who went before
was that you with your chrysalis of ore or was that me
always in your weaving wake or was that someone else
shadow of bone mystery of the finger lost in grass

……………….. SIC FATUR LACRIMANS …………….

XVI

uritur infelix Dido totaque vagatur

hiding the white space furious the city wanders
shrines and uttered vows burning unhappy
the silent wound beneath the heart nourishes
is not love the worst the shattering course of blood
through veins empty hopelessly though inflamed
a vatic phrase ensues like smoke above the mess
cannot make out what towers seem to waver
endorsed by the mad swarm in flight of bees
the Punic thrust of verse the agonic sands gather
mutilations of the fairer sex on the pyre's immobility
do fires invisible consume the ardent tongue and
shafts by Diana spent in the deepest inner soul
a woman's dire attribute sighing within deep stone
and so it goes the world under the skin consumed
ignoble pleats // if we excavate here what will we find
woods glens caves dales dells and vales soft
turf legendary boars underbrush wild vines
tangled ivy basalt imagination dying languages
or words for the hunt and sudden summer downpour
swimming in the amniotic memory of classicism
when each the other no longer memorizes the face
of dying marble threads woven in and out of verbs

the causal reference to Sirmio or Benacus poets
delving into a syntax complex with metonymy and
of course the soul-wounded queen of Carthage
recording her heart breaking songs in the desert
the afternoon we decided not to return watching
flights of birds in the sky over Volterra Etruscans
suspicious of their mirrors and backhand script
inventing an underworld not far from the gesso masks
we are given to wear to disguise our recent deaths
what anything means in the end the pleasures
we considered vital the breaths intaken and outspoken
personae umbratile figures moving in wall paintings
once bright red and the green doors portals to where
the soul cannot catch the light and voices multiple
so much and so many the various lives we have lived
now winding down to this one rock this blade of grass
this glimpse of fog shrouded moon in eternal sky
not recall? scarce few inches below the surface
find an instruction a faded illustration a warning
how can this intensity bordering on lyric madness
disassociations and pilgrimages to the holy shrines
to rivers named and unnamed promise of rebirth
asymmetrical parallels between you and me and
the lamp we shared and without falsifying identities
aching wasn't it thinking we could have had it all
gifts of the gods and the names we used playing
on the stage when evening came down unawares
dark plunging into the unknown some otherness
phantoms walking unseen parapets smoking issues
from a different sky oblique shedding faintly flares
to make out the promontory of gas shifting nightly
into the Elysian Fields were you not inside the hood
a collapsed stellar system intently viewing the maze
insane as are the half-remembered hexameters
as if hewn from a dense atmosphere of honey and
dusk the crepuscular song violet turning indigo dark

turn off the wicks smatter a few words about love
an affair lost in dreams about insect kingdoms
rites of passage across the forlorn the abandoned
as was she burning to the marrow even if only
in sequences of dactyls and spondees

I am Distance a message from Jupiter

XVII

the box that fell out of the sky
what year was that imps of protocol
will'o the wisps storm clouds hail
juggernaut of Zeus rolling pell-mell
harpies that snatch out of the heavens
moon-drunk Nymphs wagering on death
how sudden the earth seemed altered
darker than once and shadows moving
languidly serpentine over the opaque water
you wandered first from me out of the body
smitten by the allure of a strange light
emanating from the stone in the midst
of the great grasses and summer verdure
Proserpina was it come to cut a lock
of your hair ere all the heat departed
from your corporeal self a cry no less
a small indigo portion of air vivid
with sound the last of your voice
whispering bent over across the years
back to me whom you had abandoned
so much transgressed so many tears
spent on a single ivy vine now hanging
useless over that box Pandora had opened
thoughtlessly making of the world
no longer a scared place haunted by
deities of trim and glass the shining bright

but a hell hole a ditch a forensic bleed
where argument and strife the loud
and weaponry flying at raptors high
and stags leaping shot down tragically
envied by the goddess and you shoulder
to the bark earning some mead for the day
sought some loftier gyre dialoguing
with sophists dusty from their searches
for the perfect mind attributes of lamp
and brazier what small cottage heat
hard by the sump where Achilles
was supposed to have
you know the rest the circling poles
and swept waves forcing the dinghy
against the moving cliff and the Sirens
their gorgeous song atilt in the afternoon
unending sheer reflection of eternity
from under the coiling surf and pull
towards an orient of pure sand and irises
clumped around the lithe pool
Ah *frater* what were the words to that song
what the scansion and meter almost
fixed and marmoreal by which we recalled
what it was legend's Echo meant to say
sleeping as we were one inside the other
unconscious of the life surrounding
even as twilight's porphyry grazed
your brow and you tipped your head
falling forever from my gaze

XVIII

around comes Saturn's day again
rings of breath auras circling into nothing

fragments of days broken hours a shape

missing in the great circle of air

far from me the tainted   (
sections of rock crystal scattered

a shine for an instant only between the ears
lopped the flowery head falls light as dust

          -ed
moving sheds luster over the firmament

has gone lost again from memory the bright
hour the dappled dawn when rushing silently

instead the lawn spreads out in desolation
a last word a lost syllable a poem half

I am tired of *Remembering*
     it's all a metamorphosis of names
subtle alterations of sound and cue
     elided case endings memorized
irregularities
          the stuff of myth frayed
dissolving fade
the nymph Echo her face half-eaten
     by remorse
ivy tangled brain unresponsive
   to Apollo's sweetly tuned lyre

are we thus mired in the Hospital
of time? hapless legends of our
former selves   *ting ting ting!*

from Delphi news of the oracle
*"of a hard shelled tortoise being boiled
in a bronze (kettle) with the flesh of a lamb"*

---

or the monumental columns reared high
above the scorched Lands of

to read aright the inscriptions of
the just and the unjust the phonic rules

       -ing from the cliff's edge
to the roiling depths below the rocks
that *sing!*

moored to the drifting   -cution
heard just faintly the   islands's ear

vivisection of the quadrilateral space
just above the Numeral that stands for Θ

you will come to me in the dream wearing sand
for a garment and all pallid a yellow crocus
your face bursts weeping

         LABYRINTHUS oxymoron

similar phases occurred after the death of
the emperor Heliogabalus   a great Flame
consumed the sky above Syria

century after century of economic ennui
slaves running great unbounded estates
soothsayers sybils astrologers gathered
around the obelisk that points
to the midpoint of the 7th heaven

great arcs of light

all the small deaths add up until

what we see is a swarming darkness
nothing abides

I am thus heartily sick of *Remembering*
   of running the coil through its membrane
to see if the sparks light up
        amnesia and aphasia
the tongue lolling on caesuras and hiatuses

if this were indeed the end of the world
the Apocalypse and not just another eclipse
frightening the horses suddenly shadowless

a beast rears on its hind legs announcing
in an immense hoarse voice the sleep yes
the sleep unending winding like a snake
through and about the dreamers' limbs

) susurrations hissings
bong   bong fffffffffffffff

will go to Sounion for silver come morning
thence by a small one-sailed skiff to Rhodes
to see the Kolossos

and so it goes days revolving into one another
with no one aim and the body in its tepid bath
waiting for the blood to cease

not even the news from Galilee
and the life to come

promises

like bees formed in clusters at the glass
            to come in from the light

LATONA   PELOPS
hybrid associations

the lesser forms which are thoughts
and the greater ones which are ideas
and to bring to an end

to conclude what was red
fiery impulse of the unbegotten
ampersands awhirl in the deathless
so much confined to a thumbnail
thirteen moon ascendant over Pluto
lives without meaning spent
the unnamed the uncounted the

sundial spore woof antinomy
the part of the web that doesn't catch

the rest is dross the spillover from
a previous cosmos the mercurial one
of mirrors and sea-bottoms

a face talking to its half even as
night the endless

and the flowers of dreams
or insomnia

unremembered
the books lined up neatly
to form a library hyssop jasmine
lotus in blue or red
gossip of women when
the hour has struck and brown
and lavender shadows fill

the interstices in the event
of the volcano erupting or
the sea's tide gone wild
removing from the surface
the once when we stopped
to read the indictments against
and Fame the swift-winged
like a typhoon come racing
scattering rumor and strife
who was the first to plunge
the knife cutting to the quick
archipelago of ghosts

[...a waste sown with salt
image shimmering of Psyche
becoming invisible ...]

XIX

"at mihi iam puero caelestia sacra placebant"
                                                Ovid

I don't know where he is Mom
I've looked everywhere for Joe
and I can't find him

forever deeper than thought the first time
unrecorded and drawn unconscious the ships
to the sandy shores of night whilom heroes
to the death in strife dreamed other lives aloft
didn't you too fix a star just before dawn
and from it draw some lyric puzzle a color
a brightening to breathe the life to be lived
once the walls were razed and fuming columns
to the heavens sent messages never to be decoded
summers carved out of mint leaf and thyme

pools of opaque depths in which to practice
the art of reflection amidst heat's thin circularity
parenthetical woes bitter salvages heart's
constraint written enigmatically in lymph
and the multiple ampersands separating
the more than many skies each a token of fate
red the most stunning in her mysterious peplos
to you appearing as the Muse incarnate
hair shaped like the wind her oriental gaze
stones the novice in his lamp of inspiration
even as the Myrmidons swarm sleep's citadel
even as cyclopean Tiryns' turns to aphasic dust
sit by the window of the planets to read aright
the dense narrative of the walking on the Moon
how swift it all came and went the small finger
obtruding in the slender grasses of Mnemosyne
whose weave of visions enlarges and diminishes
the empty tract of mind
the empty tract of mind

Acharnians Argives Danaans Ionians et cetera
pulling the enormous simulacrum up the steep
were you within dozing recalling a humble hearth
a small flare by which you recognized your self
bluish shadow wavering in the reed-wattled hut
about to terminate the dynasties of sandy maps
that together comprised your brief existence
your brief existence
                        once in a lifetime charades
upstairs with some mimes doing *Señor Blues*
while busy in their hives the nameless scribblers
of the *Historia Augusta* fabricate and distort
the otherwise tedious sequence of *Imperatores*
mansions of oblique cases stagecraft and sorcery
doddering puppets reciting Etruscan auguries
in a relentless storm of spittle and rebukes

but why deepen the chasm more with rants
history's poor cloth faded and moth consumed
flying rag on a broken fog shrouded mast
when is a man happiest?
what matter the many thousand waters
whence Legend displays its myriad glassy vowels?
what is the difference between the *first* time
and the time when it suddenly makes no sense?
pitched into the eerie mere guarded by barkless dogs
in pharaonic masks make mystery of the moonlight
where we go revolving ceaselessly in enigmatic trance
waking and not waking to other lives
sometimes a tyrant in a wave of ire and munificence
others a helot drubbed for losing at the race
what is the puzzle that keeps its buzz?
head tossed to endless stone the eye does its thing
seeing everything it could ever be in a trice
then blindly returns to its sovereign god
the small entity perched like a gnat upon a mote
whose entire rationale is to deny the *ghost*

why did you set the oxen loose and leave
the plow in the field, Slaves?

a certain sophist taught me mathematics
and the heavens opened
the urge to mysticism & violent outbursts of madness
sowing salt in the Elysian Fields a votary
breast bared to the goddess in her Transcendence
pure hands and a soul conscious of no evil
yet spent many a noon hour smoking in the court
and looking wantonly on the Nymphs in passing
confusion was great and the temptations
in the spring night air odor of fresh manure and lilac
when will it ever come back?
twenty or thirty worlds manifest in the Holy!

what's to worry about this knot?
riddle me this, Joe
when is a man happiest?

he's probably hiding in the downstairs closet
you know how he likes to scare us

"et sit humus cineri non onerosa tuo"

XX

CAELESTIA SACRA

parenthetical clauses containing the discards of language
(*Phoebus his western flare has grazed thy temple*
speech acts that violate   )
more beautiful yet the moon as inscribed
on the back of a mother-of-pearl mind
the meaning of *lyric* the song of the skin
stretched out on its lyre the music ineffable
nostalgia for the multiple losses sustained breathing
great wingèd beings assuming poses of marble
becoming blind statuary riddling the causeways
among them you laced with a laurel frond
Daphne stone incarnate elevating to a higher gyre
transforming the verdant into a symposium of flame
the godhead has touched you again and again
and turning to us your mute appeals your Eyes
and whatever they see the ruins of a gone world
remnants of sand and vowels ignited by the Lamp
what can no longer be maintained by memory
slipping away into so many green islets
it aches at the base where feet used to touch earth
or somewhere in mid air where noon originates
fiercely yellow and withering far from Echo
tracing her vagaries across the lintel of sleep

as if dew were the alphabet of all secrets
or this is the occasional reprise of syntax
woven and embroidered symptom of illusion
and desire the levitation of matter in dreams
madness to be otherwise in the far otherwhere
out there in the round of gyres where Apollo
steadies his aim and exercises love's mount
what language cannot contain and the whiteness
the multiple that blinds like a melody of the unspeakable
hitherto the grasses with their many small ears
and the shepherd's pipe and longing itself
the yearning for afternoons in the beyond of zero
when body mingled with body in the unconscious
sweat like ingots of liquid gold striating the *anima*
in its puerperal fever to flee the dross of existence
so many instants like pinpricks of light
and inspiration with its fantastic waxen wings
aloft in the surfeit of ether burning its Hour
how will we ever read the Poem in another language?
and Daphne her nerve-ends of hyacinth and anemone
swiftly losing all sense as if the hundred waters
of Myth were loosed in a single shower
hair and leaf and stone and lip absolved
what else is there to say about this metamorphosis
this acclimatizing of ivy to the subterranean
to the single chthonic deity of the Irreversible

(the harp pandemonium the infrequencies of sound
the nevertheless and the verisimilitudes sighing
deep the soughing in invisible trees chance to meet
and part and never see again a whenever a flux
dying to the mouth a shivering a river beneath
taking the all to its nether unit lightless glade
ruled by Pluto's child bride the indwelling cosmic
the viol rapt and chaste the at once and No
whoever is at the door knocking nightly daimon

whizzing in the Ear and rock married to rock and
violence to the unutterable syllable whatever
happening and not occurring and becoming and
not being the hand to its other the shoulder bearing
all the drama of breath and suddenness corruption
pallid faces withdrawing into the Unseen)

caelestia sacra
the whispered final words

EPILOGUE

the Great Bear the Lesser Bear the Wagon
the starry pelt of Orion the Wheel
the liquid alphabets of the comets
the isthmus of Corinth Berenice's lock
Diana's blood red moon Daphne's martyrdom
Cadmus and the opaque stones of Thebes
the monumental secrets of Calypso
the ordinal & cardinal rites of the Etruscans
the naked and mental shoulder of Minerva
the seven suspended poems & the Banquet
the Holy year of ten thousand months
the march up-country through Asia Minor
deadly encounters with the Basilisk & Adonis
whose river empties in the watery Circle
the surf and zone of Aphrodite
the owl of Athene & ox-eyed Hera
sister and bride to Zeus of the Golden shower
the swans whose flight is a white writing
the Hesperides the floating islands of the West
the cattle of the sun grazing on eternity's flank
the grassy empire of the Cyclops
planets and Ideas of the world in the Mint
Cyrus Darius Xerxes engraved in brazen ether
the storms of the Oak tree and the Academy

wars of infinite length fought over the Bride
legends dark and hazy of the Ganges
where ascetics bathed in ruddy lymph
predict the Cataclysm & the Dew
the Baedekker of Heaven writ in pyramid script
and all the sands burning underfoot
burying the palimpsests and the Papyrus
the Stygian caverns and the black fruit of Pluto
Persephone and the weeping of the dead
shades and shadows of nameless Heroes
the journey to the book of the Sybil
the Golden Bough and the Key to the Underworld
vast hexameters of marmoreal verse
blank and thorough as the Olympian Realm !

FORSAN ET HAEC OLIM MEMINISSE IUVABIT

Berkeley CA   01/11/15-02/13/15

Other titles by
Ivan Argüelles/
Published by
Luna Bisonte Prods:

FIAT LUX [2014]

A DAY IN THE SUN [2012]

ULTERIOR VISION(S) [2011]

Additional copies of this book
and of the above listed titles
are available at:

https://www.lulu.com/lunabisonteprods